The Rez
Road Follies

The Rez Road Follies

Canoes,

Casinos,

Computers, and

Birch Bark Baskets

JIM NORTHRUP

University of Minnesota Press
Minneapolis

To my wife, Patricia, Umpa Owastewe, Patty,

Red Tail Hawk Woman, and Pat

Copyright 1997 by Jim Northrup

First published in hardcover by Kodansha America, Inc., 1997
First University of Minnesota Press edition, 1999

Published by the University of Minnesota Press
111 Third Avenue South, Suite 290
Minneapolis, MN 55401-2520
http://www.upress.umn.edu

Library of Congress Cataloging-in-Publication Data

Northrup, Jim, 1943–
The Rez Road follies : canoes, casinos, computers, and birch bark baskets / Jim Northrup.
p.   cm.
ISBN 0-8166-3495-5 (pbk.)
1. Northrup, Jim, 1943–   . 2. Ojibwa Indians Biography.
3. Ojibwa Indians — Social life and customs. 4. Ojibwa wit and humor. 5. Fond du Lac Indian Reservation (Minn.) — Social life and customs. I. Title.
[E99.C6N67   1999]
818'.5409 — dc21
[B]
99-30701

Printed in the United States of America on acid-free paper

The University of Minnesota is an equal-opportunity educator and employer.

11 10 09 08 07 06 05 04   10 9 8 7 6 5 4

CONTENTS

....

Families

NINDANAWEMAAGANAG

FAMILIES ARE ONE of the blessings of the Anishinaabeg. Living without family would be like trying to live without air and water. It can be done but not for very long. I live on the Fond du Lac Reservation in northern Minnesota with my extended family. We are an island of Anishinaabeg in the surrounding sea of what is now called America. In Rez slang, we call ourselves Shinnobs. We have been called Chippewa, Ojibwe, Indians, Blanket Asses, Bow and Arrows, and "you people."

My wife, Patricia, grandson Ezigaa, sometimes a dog but never a cat, make up my current household. In years past, our five grown children have returned to the nest. We have been successful in pushing them back out into the world. Cousins and friends are always stopping by to share or learn new gossip. Our friends and relatives from urban America report they sleep longer when they visit the quiet village of Sawyer.

I used to be known as a bullshitter but that didn't pay anything. I began calling myself a storyteller—a little better, more prestige—but it still didn't pay anything. I became a freelance writer. At first it was more free than lance, then I started getting money for my words. But, when I became an author, I began charging consultant's fees.

Any author's voice resonates with words, phrases, and events from the past. One way to find out something is to ask questions. Questions, like families, help make sense of the twists and turns of life. They highlight the humor we're blessed with. They are linguistic tricksters; sometimes the shape of the question shifts before you get the answer, then you see the subject in a new way. I'll admit I have a questioning habit. Each month in my Fond du Lac Follies column, or whenever I think we need to meditate on an answer, I'll ask and answer a question like this:

Are you a full-blooded Indian?

No, I'm a pint low, just came from the blood bank.

Or,

Do you speak your language?

Yup, yours too.

Or,

Do you people still live in ponies and ride teepees?

Nope, never did.

My relatives, *Nindanawemaaganag*, are part of the turning cycle of generations. I am just one of the generations of Anishinaabeg that have lived on this continent. We have a great flood story like the Bible or the Gilgamesh epic. Our story was being told long before the Bible or the epic came to this land. I have heard the old stories and continue to tell new ones.

I heard some of the stories from my four grandparents. I can trace my family trees back to 1740, 1750, 1787, and 1825.

When I turned fifty in 1993, I paused in my usual reporterly column to reintroduce myself. I thought it was time since I was, to quote the title the editors gave the column, "almost an elder." I am finally at the age where it doesn't matter if my belly bulges a bit. No matter how many sit-ups I do, the bulge is still there. I did one just the other week, it didn't change a thing.

When I was young, I used to hear the average age of death for Indians was forty-four years. I adopted an attitude that anything over that many years was pure gravy, just juice. It was a bonus for trying to live a good life.

I was born during World War II. My parents, Bope and Mawinz, Jim and Alice Northrup, were born on the Fond du Lac Reservation. Both grew up here in Sawyer and this is where they chose to live. Dad, an auto mechanic, was hospitalized for tuberculosis and spent some years away from home. Ma held the family together during his absences. They must have gotten together a few times because I have eleven younger brothers and sisters, as well as an older sister, Judy.

Judy and I were exposed to tuberculosis because almost everyone near us had the disease. We spent some months in the TB sanitarium at *Agwajiing,* on a different reservation. I don't remember much but do recall my days were spent playing outside and my nights were spent sleeping in a crib. I could wave at my sister across the hospital hallway. After a few months we were sent home.

When we got home we went to stay with relatives. Judy went to live with my mother's parents, Mike and Susan Shabiash. I went to live with my paternal grandmother, Angeline. We were told the old people liked having kids around. That was part of it, I am sure, but another reason we stayed with them was because our grandparents had food.

I remember my grandmother, Angeline, taking me to downtown Duluth to watch the victory parade that signaled the end of World War II. My uncles Stun, Rob, Ole, and Hayman came home, telling stories about places like France, North Africa, and the South Pacific.

Shortly after the war, Judy and I were sent to a federal boarding school at Pipestone, Minnesota. I do remember wondering why just Indians went away to school. I asked Ma why the white kids didn't have to leave home when they were in the first grade. She couldn't answer, she just looked away, but not before I saw the pain in her eyes.

Judy and I got on the yellow school bus that was making the circuit of the northern Minnesota Indian communities. The bus was full of Anishinaabeg children from the other reservations. We were the last to be picked up for the trip to Pipestone in southern Minnesota. Both Judy and I thought we were off on a grand adventure.

We were separated as soon as we got off the bus. I remember waving to her as she was walking away to the girls' dorm. We met our matron and were shown where we would sleep.

The dormitory was a huge room with rows and rows of beds. I remember the smell of urine and disinfectant. Some adult washed our heads with kerosene and we were given a tablespoon of cod-liver oil.

As I recall, our days went something like this. We woke up and made our beds. After that we went downstairs to clean up and get dressed for the day. We formed squads and marched down the sidewalks to the dining hall. The first meal was a brutal learning experience. While I was eating, a big guy reached across and took most of my food. It didn't take me long to learn how to eat while guarding my food. I put one arm around my tray and ate with my fork in a stabbing position.

After cleaning the dormitory, we went to school. School was easy for me and I quickly skipped a grade and caught up with my sister. She didn't like that too much so she taught me about cottonwood trees. Judy explained that we get cotton from those trees. She said if I was lucky I could find a new shirt or something hanging from the branches. I spent weeks looking at cottonwood trees before I caught on. In the classroom I learned where cotton really comes from.

The time outside the classroom was spent in fighting. I was one of the youngest and smallest so I got a daily beating from the big guys. I quickly learned how to fight back because crying wasn't working. Along the way, I learned that if I didn't cry, I might even win the fight. I was in thirty-seven fights by the time Halloween came. I won two of them.

One day I got into an argument with a boy in my

class. We fought after our noon meal. I won the fight because I made him cry before he made me cry. The boy told his older brother about the fight. The older brother, who was two grades ahead of us, told me we would fight after school. I was scared the whole afternoon. Finally the time to fight came. I was really scared and fought as hard as I could. I ignored my swollen lips and bloody nose and kept swinging. I was too scared to cry. The fight seemed to last a long time and after I got in a lucky punch, the bigger boy started to cry. I kept punching because I was still scared. Some big guys dragged me off and told me I had won the fight. The second brother told a third brother who was three grades ahead of us. I was able to get in two punches before the third brother pounded me into the ground.

I learned how to get up diplomatically after being beaten into the ground. I lost so many fights that I got tired of crying and began getting up afterward instead. I would find something to look at directly in front of me. It didn't matter what it was. Outside, it was a blade of grass or a stick. Inside, I learned to study the cracks in the concrete floor or the pattern of the wood grain. I would pretend great interest in the object, poking at it with a finger. Then I would have to look at it from another angle until I was up on my knees. Finally, I would get to my feet, still looking. I would then kick the object and walk away as if I had lost interest in it. It doesn't take long to get from your knees to your feet. I developed a survival strategy when being chased by a big guy. When I would see I couldn't outrun him, I would drop to the ground and ball up, tripping the big guy. I would then get up and quickly run in the opposite direction.

The nights in the boys' dormitory were the worst. After the night guard woke up the piss ants—those who usually wet their beds—we would try to sleep. Sometimes you could hear a big guy crawling into bed with a younger boy.

A young one on the little guys' side of the dormitory would begin quietly crying. Maybe he was crying because he was lonely and homesick, maybe he had been assaulted by a big guy. Whatever the reason, the boys on either side of him would tell him to be quiet. When the little guy wouldn't quit crying, the ones next to him would be reminded how homesick they were and start crying also. We could hear the wave of crying start at one end of the dormitory and come traveling down until the boy next to you was crying and you were sobbing also. I suspect all the boys were crying because it was the only thing we could do. After a night like that, we all got up in the morning and pretended that it didn't happen.

I didn't know how to write that first year. Pauline Moose used to write my "Dear Ma, How are you? I am fine" letters for me. I will always remember her kindness. Judy didn't know much more than I did about letter writing.

After a couple of months in the first grade at Pipestone, I decided I'd had enough of this boarding school business. I wanted to go home. There was always talk around the school about runaways so I thought I'd try. I told Judy about my plan. She tried to talk me out of it but couldn't. Judy reminded me that we came to the school on Highway 23; if I just headed north, I would eventually get home. She walked me to the rear gate of the school. As Judy was waving good-bye, she asked me to tell Ma to send her some candy when I got home.

I started walking right after breakfast. I followed the Highway 23 signs north. I enjoyed the freedom of that bright, sunny day. The thought of going home kept me putting one foot in front of the other. After a couple hours of walking, I found a hawk's foot on the side of the road. What a treasure, I thought. No one else I knew owned a hawk foot. I picked it up and thought of showing my family what came with me on my long walk home. It smelled a little ripe but I didn't mind because now I had company.

It was getting close to dark when I heard a loud noise behind me. It was a big, black car sliding to a stop on the gravel shoulder. The doors flew open and two big people got out and started running toward me. I turned and ran for the cornfield. They chased me up and down the rows of corn. I even used my fall-down–ball-up trick once before they caught me and dragged me to the car. On the ride back to the school, one of the white men told me I had made it nine miles. That's when they noticed my smell. One man dug into my pocket and took out my hawk foot. He threw it in the ditch. I don't remember the beating I got back at the school but do remember feeling bad about the hawk foot.

Judy was happy to see me back. She let me have a big bite of our maple sugar cake right away. We would get packages from home that always contained maple sugar cakes. Judy and I would take tiny bites and make the cake last until the next one came. We knew the cakes were from Gramma Shabiash and her sugar bush. The taste always brought us home.

Finally, we were finished with school for the year. We rode home on the same yellow school bus. We went to all the other reservations before we got to ours. Once we were home, I told my Ma how I got slapped for using an Ojibwe expression. She swore in English at the white matron who was three hundred miles away. Our parents and grandparents spoke only English during our summer at home.

The second, third, and fourth grades were easier because my cousin, Punkin Blacketter, transferred from another boarding school. I had backing and I didn't have to fight as often. We played hard. The quarry at Pipestone was like a magnet to the young boys of the school. Pipestone is a red rock that can be carved into pipes and other objects. This is one of the few places in North America where such stone can be found. We tried our hand at carving the pipestone, using a piece of glass to drill and shape the stone. One afternoon we planned on sneaking off to the quarry for more stone. Right after school we went out to the playground. While everyone else was playing, we sauntered over and casually dropped into a cornfield ditch. Once out of sight, we began crawling. Punkin was in front and I crawled right into his boots when he stopped. While crawling backward, he yelled, "Snake!"

He had crawled nose to nose with a large bull snake. We grabbed the snake and forgot about the quarry. We jumped up and started chasing girls around with the snake. When we had scared everyone we could, we returned the snake to the cornfield.

Federal boarding school wasn't a totally negative experience. I learned how to survive some terrible things. I learned how to fight even when scared. Most important, I learned how to read and write English.

In the 1950s, when I was a teenager, my relatives and I went to a Christian boarding school in South Dakota. Brainerd Indian Training School was run by the Wesleyan Methodists. It was fun outwitting the teachers and preachers. We didn't respect those who gave their lives to minister to the godless heathens. As a heathen, I understood it would be easier to feed my brothers and sisters if Judy and I ate with the Christians for a few months. This boarding school was a lark compared to Pipestone.

The school was situated in the southern part of the Black Hills. The campus was in a valley between two hills. We would spend hours carrying tires to the top of the hills so we could roll them down across the campus. There were contests to see whose tire would go the farthest, whose would jump the highest. Truck tires were the best for our purposes. After the fun was over, we would have to pay. I atoned for my sins by using a pick and shovel to dig many, many ditches.

We were given heavy doses of Christianity. We went to church twice on Sunday, prayer meeting every Wednesday night, and an hour of morning devotions every day. The school livened things up by inviting touring revival groups to the campus. Then we heathens went to church every night for three weeks. The Christianity didn't stick and we returned to the Reservation and our heathen ways. I came home with tales of the Holy Wars.

After graduating from Carlton Public high school in 1961, I enlisted in the United States Marine Corps. I knew from the old stories that the Anishinaabeg were warriors and my family expected me to be one. In 1965, the Marines landed in Vietnam. I joined India Company, Third Battalion, Ninth Marines in September of that same year. After thirteen months in-country, I returned with my own war stories to tell.

My two oldest sons, Jim and Matthew, were born during the Vietnam War. I remember feeling they shouldn't have to fight in a war because I had done it. Nobody hates war as much as someone who has been in one. The rest of our blended family includes Tony, Calvin, Dolly, Joseph, and Heather.

My family suffered during the Gulf War. Matthew was in the U.S. Army then and I was worried he might have to fight and die. He didn't have to go and we were relieved when it was over.

For a few years, I had just three grandchildren: Ezigaa (Aaron), Mato (Mato) and Niiwin (James). At first, I thought I was too young to be sleeping with a Gramma. I would look around for my own Grampa when the kids called me that. After hearing it every day for three years, I started believing it. Now I grab Ezigaa's hand and tell him he can go to the store with Grampa. Patricia and I currently have eight grandchildren: Wiigwaas, Noonah, Zhashagi, Haapi,and Gwiiwizens are the youngest. They have English names but I prefer calling them names we have given them.

I wonder what the future holds for them and the coming generations of Anishinaabeg?

When I was in my physical prime, I'd start running and be at top speed in a step or two. Over the years, I've noticed it takes longer and longer to get there. Right now, it takes an hour and a half. By that time, I have forgotten why I wanted to run in the first place. As I get older, I find fewer and fewer reasons to run at full speed.

Do you have an exercise program?

Yes, I cough from the Camels and do deep knee bends when picking up nickels I drop at the casino.

Now that I am getting close to becoming an elder, I look around to see all the things I have yet to learn. I am hoping to learn from my elders and grandchildren. I could be called a junior elder, maybe an apprentice elder.

Everywhere I go it seems that people have questions about me and the Anishinaabeg. Some of the questions are about who I am.

Are you really an Indian?

No, I'm a spirit. I just look real to you.

Or,

Do Indians have psychic powers?

I knew you were going to ask me that, I just knew it.

Or,

What tribe are you from?

I'm half Ojibwe, half Chippewa, and the rest is Anishinaabeg.

Or,

How long have you been Indian?

Fifty-two years. It would have been fifty-three but I was sick a year.

Or,

Why is the white man in such a hurry to get to Mars?

They think we have land there.

It continues. One of the best reasons to write questions is to get answers out there so we are not such specimens to society. The questions are sometimes serious, sometimes silly, but mostly fun.

Jeez, did you boogid (fart)*?*

No, we're downwind of the paper mill.

Or,

Why do Shinnobs make better lovers?

A lot of them don't have to get up and go to work in the morning.

When I wrote that question in my column, I got a letter from some fellow Shinnobs who had to get up and go to work. They thought I was contributing to a negative stereotype. I ran their letter in the next column, which gave me a chance to repeat the question.

Or,

What breed are you?

> Pure Northrup. 100 percent frybread/wild rice/
> maple syrup–propelled, a ricing, basketmaking,
> storytelling Shinnob.

I am my father's son and my children's father and only the government counts my blood in fractions. Fractions, like taxes, have changed over the years of my life. When I first heard about blood quantum, I was labeled fifteen-sixteenths Minnesota Chippewa Indian. When I graduated from high school and was checking on scholarships, I was thirteen-sixteenths. The last time I checked, I was eleven-sixteenths. I quit checking because I am losing my blood somewhere.

Questions and answers are scattered across days, events, places, and stories. The family stories we tell help hold us together.

I like gathering my kids and their kids around to tell family stories. One winter evening I told them a when-I-was-young kind of story. It was a part of the history of the family, of the Anishinaabeg.

Being the oldest boy in the family gave me certain advantages. I automatically went along when the car ride was over fifty miles. I thought I was the favorite son riding with Ma and Dad. I didn't know Dad wanted me along so that I could walk for help when the car broke down. I did get to hear a lot of stories though.

On one trip we went to the next Reservation on tribal business. My Dad was on the Tribal Executive Committee. The Shinnob politicians were meeting to determine whether they should change the eligibility requirements for enrollment in the Minnesota Chippewa Tribe. My Ma and I sat with the other family members in the rented hall in Bemidji, Minnesota. Representatives from six Chippewa reservations in Minnesota gathered to hear testimony on the question of lowering the blood quantum level from one-half to one-fourth.

Testimony from the Bureau of Indian Affairs employees droned on all morning. The first speaker spoke, then introduced the second speaker, who did the same thing. Same with the third.

After listening all morning, the Tribal Executive Committee broke for lunch and some drank alcohol while eating. It was later said that some drank more than they ate.

The meeting resumed in the upstairs hall.

During the course of the first bureaucrat's testimony, he used the phrase "25 percent" in discussing the issue of blood quantum level.

Then I heard a chair scrape on the floor; a representative of the people stood up. He slammed his hand down on the table three times and when there was silence, said, "Wait a minute, wait a minute here. I got something to say. All morning long you people were talking about one-fourth. One-fourth this and one-fourth that. Now this afternoon you start talking about 25 percent. Why did you change it? I want to know, the people of my Reservation want to know, why you changed from one-fourth to 25 percent."

The bureaucrat who was testifying started looking down through his notes. Other representatives began looking out the window. One nodded to another who threw his eyeballs over his shoulder in shame.

The silence in the room was broken by the man's wife urgently whispering to him in Ojibwe. He looked at her, then at the bureaucrat, and said, "Never mind."

Then he sat down.

My Ma and Dad told and retold that story eight times on the ride home. I was in the backseat, listening and practicing, listening and practicing.

A lot of our family stories revolve around kids and dogs. My youngest son, Joseph, had a "combat" cornet. He has wanted to be a musician since he was banging on pots and pans as a toddler.

He got his chance when the school announced that fifth graders could now join band. The boy thought about it and had trouble deciding which instrument to play. At first, he wanted a saxophone because the oldest girl plays one on "The Simpsons." He later decided on the cornet.

It was a long week of waiting for him after we signed the rental papers. Finally, Tuesday came and he could pick up the instrument. He jumped off the school bus and skipped home carrying the black case that held the cornet. The family members gathered around as he unsnapped the case to show us the shiny horn nestled inside the velvet case. He proudly identified the different parts, the mouthpiece, the water valve, the valves that control the sound. He even tried to get some music out of the shiny cornet. At the risk of stunting his growth as a musician, I suggested he go next door to show the neighbors how it sounded.

The folks next door were impressed and gave him a lot of encouragement to continue learning the cornet. Their son, a stocky seventy-pound ball of fire, didn't know what was happening. All he knew was his friend Joseph was visiting with a new toy. He came running out of the bedroom and jumped in Joseph's lap. The new musician was holding the cornet in his lap. The horn was crushed between the two boys.

Joseph showed me the damaged instrument. The bell part of the horn was bent at a ninety-degree angle. It looked like the cornet was trying to look over its right shoulder. I tried to make him feel better by telling him he could now play the horn around corners. I told him he had the only combat cornet in town.

Joseph's music career remains on hold until we hear what happens when he faces the music dude at school. I told him I wouldn't want to be standing in his Nikes when that happens. He didn't say anything, he just went outside to play with his dog.

We're kind of tough on dogs. Some stay a day and others are around for a year or more. We go through them like some casinos go through managers. Our current dog is named Outside. Ezigaa named him. Now he can stand at the front door and say, "Inside, Outside" or "Outside, Outside."

Then there was Frybread. He was the same size and color as a piece of frybread. He was also the right size for an owl Happy Meal. I think that is what happened to him.

Concrete was the product of a broken marriage. Neither partner wanted custody of the dog when the marriage failed, so the big golden retriever came north to live with us on the Reservation. Since he was a city dog, he preferred sleeping on the front steps made of concrete. Thus he named himself. In the coldest weather, he slept on the concrete. He refused offers of a dog house, a sheltered spot under the canoe, or even inside. Concrete just laid on the front steps and protected the house.

When not on duty, Concrete liked to ride in the car. It didn't matter where he was going, he just liked to ride. While riding, Concrete would stick his head out the window, a goofy look on his face as he sampled the passing odors. His ears were windblown as he sniffed the country air.

One day I had to go somewhere. "Get in," I told the tail-wagging dog. Concrete jumped in and took up his place in the backseat.

I had to stop because I recognized my brother's car on the side of the road. The hood was up and Vern was gazing at the car's innards. I let the dog out to run around while we got Vern's car going. It just needed a jump start to get it roaring on its own. When we were done, I opened the door for the dog.

"Get in." A big golden blur jumped in the car.

When we got home, I opened the back door and said, "Get out."

The dog jumped out and went tail-wagging toward the house.

I looked closer at the dog. He didn't look right. I said, "Concrete, where did you get that collar?" He didn't have one on before we started our little trip.

"Who put it on you?" I knew he couldn't have done it himself.

"Concrete, you gained weight, and who put that blond streak in your fur?"

This wasn't Concrete, it was some other golden retriever, an impostor. I asked him what he had done to my dog. He didn't answer. I went back to the car, opened the back door and said, "Get in."

The strange dog jumped in the car.

I drove back to the scene of the crime. There was Concrete sitting patiently on the side of the road. When he saw the familiar car, he started wagging his tail. Concrete was squealing with excitement. I stopped the car, opened the back door, and said, "Get out."

The fake Concrete leaped out.

I pointed at Concrete with my finger and said, "You, get in."

Concrete licked my hand on his way into the car. We drove home and when we got there, I said, "Get out."

Concrete walked up to the front steps and laid down on the concrete.

He died one winter when he and a snowplow tried to be in the same place at the same time.

We can't tell family dog stories without mentioning Speed Bump. I forgot the name we gave him when he came to live with us. His name changed after an accident on the gravel road. We were just coming home from somewhere.

The dog was so happy to see us that he ran under the car. I hit the brakes and slid. I felt the front wheel of the heavy Buick pass up and over my dog. Oh no, I thought, I killed my dog. Then I could hear him thumping under the car. My dog was still alive. I turned the steering

wheel carefully and slowly backed up. I felt the front
wheel pass up and over my dog again.

When he was finally clear of the car, he took off howl-
ing for the woods. He didn't come home for three days,
but when he did, he had a new name—Speed Bump.

We've tried different sizes, different breeds. Most were
mixed but their end was the same. They died so we
could get to know a new dog.

Rats, someone stole Outside. My cousin, Rathide, reported seeing a stranger in a strange car stop on the
road in front of our house. The dognapper opened the
car door, snatched Outside, and drove off at a low rate
of speed. My cousin couldn't describe the driver but did
say the car was kind of new, brown, maybe blue or one
of those other colors. He was positive it had Minnesota
license plates though.

Outside was a friendly dog and probably thought he
was going to get some food or a rub on the head. Outside didn't know about dog thieves.

My grandson Ezigaa was angry, then sad. We tried to
console him and explain about dog thieves. His brown
eyes were full of tears when he said, "I know, I know, but
I just want my dog back."

We took my cousin for a ride to see if he could spot
the car that was involved in the dognapping. We drove
in an expanding circle around the house. Nothing, no
sign of the car or the dog. It looked like another case for
Robert Stack and "Unsolved Mysteries."

Now we have new dogs. My wife Patricia went to visit
her relatives on the Lower Sioux Reservation and came
back with a little puppy.

He is a biter—his little needle teeth snag socks, pants
legs, and even moccasins. Because of our tough dog

luck, we didn't want to name him right away. When it looked like he would last a while we started calling him Toenail and I don't know why. He just reminded someone of a toenail. He is mostly black except for the silver paint he got when he was watching them paint the liquid propane gas tank. Ezigaa was calling him Duct Tape for a while but it didn't stick.

My wife went to visit her relatives again. Toenail was joined by another puppy. This one is a full-blooded poodle but the only papers he has are on the floor. He is a small, brown ball of fur. He looks like someone left the perm in too long. I have avoided the little land mines he leaves. Ezigaa named him Inside but because of the way everyone steps on him, I want to name him Floor. My wife is talking about visiting her relatives again. I'd put my foot down but . . .

And the notorious Northrup dog luck continues.

Ezigaa continues to be a good Grampa teacher. He has been living with us since he was a week old. His mother, Dolly, calls him Aaron. We called him Air and Water for a while because we thought he had environmental leanings. Now we call him Ezigaa. It means wood tick in Ojibwe and it describes the way he hugs. Sometimes we call him Your Royal Highness and once in a while *AARON*.

He is just discovering the world. I feel young seeing the world through his eyes. He gets up early so he can old-man around with his Grampa. He comes into the room and greets me with open arms. Still sleepy, he climbs in my lap and we sit for a few minutes, feeling each other's heartbeat. We call it the Morning Ezigaa

Hug. Then together we look around the yard to see if
night has changed anything. Without saying anything,
we watch the birds flying by. We both turn to hear the
train passing through downtown Sawyer.

As a Grampa, I get the joys of parenthood without the
wet diaper part. I've got the family convinced that
Grampas are exempt from diaper duties.

Ezigaa and I share a walk almost every day. We go
looking for rocks and find memories. The gravel roads
of Sawyer are blessed with a generous splash of agates.
I don't know what geological age formed the stones but
I do know a pretty rock when I see one.

It is easy for Ezigaa to find agates because he is built
so close to the ground. He finds even the smallest agates,
some the size of a pinhead. His eye identifies the lines of
color the Creator pressed together. Centuries of light,
sand, and minerals mixed together to make these small
signatures my grandson picks out. He hands me what he
finds and I examine them closely. When I finally declare
them to be agates, he laughs and takes them to the con-
tainer where we store our treasures. He sometimes drops
them on the way and has to find them a second time.
Ezigaa now knows the difference between agate, quartz,
and flint.

I remember my Ma or Gramma walking down these
same roads looking for maybe the same agates. While
walking with them, I couldn't understand what agates
had to do with the trip. I always wanted to get to where
we were going. Now that I am older, I realize that the
journey is as much a part of the trip as the destination.
I still remember the praise I got when I found a good
agate.

Ezigaa knows the best time for agate hunting is after

the road grader has gone by. I don't know what we will do with our pile of pretty rocks. For now, we just take them out to look at when it is too dark or rainy to find more. The translucent red rocks are fascinating for a little boy and his Grampa.

When not hunting agates, we sometimes take a road trip to widen our circle. We once motored to the Red Cliff Reservation in northern Wisconsin to visit friends. While packing rations for the trip, I remembered trips with Gramma. Chips and cookies were in our rations. We had a jug of Sawyer water and a Thermos of coffee. A Hershey candy bar rounded out our supplies.

It was a warm day with a light breeze. We decided it was sweatshirt weather, not quite jacket weather but too cool for T-shirts. Ezigaa and I motored along the south shore of Lake Superior. We were following no schedule so we stopped everywhere to look at things a little closer. One of Ezigaa's choices was a beach. We got out of the car and walked in the soft sand. The sand slowed us down so we looked at everything a little closer. We studied an orange and black ladybug that was resting above the high water mark.

Ezigaa's feet were beginning to drag on the way back to the car so I carried him. His eyes were closing as I buckled the seat belt around him. Later, when he woke up, I gave him a drink of Sawyer water. He went back to his post of pointing out birds, cows, and yellow school buses.

When we reached our destination, I visited while Ezigaa explored a new backyard. While driving home on Highway 2, I realized I couldn't always guide his adventures but it was nice to make a small circle through life together.

Ezigaa's Gramma cares for many of the details of his life also. Women from all over the Reservation have their hands across several generations. Some because their daughters started new families early, some because they extended their own families across more than one decade. Parenting advice is not hard to come by in Sawyer or the rest of the Reservation. As great as it is for women to have families, there is a shadow in our history.

For many years, the United States government had a policy of termination regarding Indian people. The U.S. wanted to get out of the Indian business. It is an attitude that lingered long after its formal abolishment.

As a result many Indian women have been sterilized. Some were coerced, some were paid, and most were encouraged to have their fallopian tubes severed. Whatever the reason or method, the results have been the same: barren women and fewer black-haired, brown-eyed babies.

In my column, the Fond du Lac Follies, I have written about the anesthetized feeling our culture bears by talking about one man, one woman, and one hope. I wrote about how they took a trip to springtime where hope for a new life seemed possible.

For her, it was a chance to feel whole again. For him, it was a chance to start a new family. The husband and wife decided to reverse the sterilization through a form of micro-surgery called reanastomis. In talking with friends and relatives, she learned of six others who wanted to try the new procedue. One of the women heard it could be done at an Indian Service Hospital.

The only drawback was that the hospital was eight hundred miles away.

Preparing for the surgery took months. She had a physical exam, blood tests, and her ovulation cycle was identified. She had barium X rays and was counseled. Her fifteen-year dream was about to become a reality.

She spoke with the doctor from the OB-GYN department and sent him her medical history for evaluation. He decided she was a good candidate for the procedure. An appointment was made at the IHS hospital in Claremore, Oklahoma. Since this was considered optional surgery, the costs were borne by the couple.

As they drove south from northern Minnesota, the snowbanks got smaller and smaller. By the time they got to Iowa, the snow was completely gone. As they continued south, green grass and birds were seen. The birds were robins and red tail hawks. The couple interpreted this as a good sign because her name in the Dakota language is Red Tail Hawk Woman.

The weather cleared and the northern Minnesota Indians began to shed their layers of winter clothing. By the time they passed through Missouri, he was down to a T-shirt and blue jeans.

They arrived in Claremore and checked into the hospital. While filling out the forms, she talked about the operation that had severed her fallopian tubes. She said Indian women used to talk about the operation that paid them one hundred dollars. She thought it was part of the social service delivery system. At that time, in the early '70s, no one counseled her or told her she would have a longing for children or yearn to feel complete as a woman.

They met the doctor who explained the procedure

using charts, diagrams, and X rays. He talked openly about the dangers inherent in any surgery. He explained that she had a 10 percent chance of a tubal pregnancy because of the scar tissue. However, the doctor said, she would have a 50 percent chance of getting pregnant after the surgery. She smiled and squeezed her husband's hand because right now she had a 0 percent chance of conceiving. The doctor said he had performed the same surgical procedure seven times in the last year.

When they walked into the room on the surgical ward, they met a nurse they knew from the Reservation back home. Oklahoma wasn't full of strangers anymore. She gave them a brief history of Claremore and suggested an economical motel for the husband.

On the morning of the surgery, an anesthesiologist came into her room and talked about the method they would be using. The couple was mentally prepared for the surgery.

At eleven o'clock, her long black hair was tucked into a surgical cap and she was wheeled into the operating room. Three hours and two packs of cigarettes later, the husband learned from the doctor that the operation was a success.

She spent a half hour in the recovery room. She had a catheter, an IV, and a small bandage on her abdomen. She also had reconnected fallopian tubes. When the husband told his wife the operation was a success, her eyes filled with happy tears. They held each other for a long time. She still felt the effects of the surgery and sedative and was sleepy. She slept and he ran out to call the family back home in Minnesota to report on the surgery.

The next day, the catheter was removed and she was encouraged to get up and move around to prevent blood clots. The doctor explained about the dissolving stitches inside the incision. Five days after she checked in, the doctor removed the staples and gave her a final checkup. He gave the couple instructions about her recovery: No lifting for six weeks, no driving for two weeks, and frequent stops to walk around on the way back home to Minnesota.

When the couple arrived back in Minnesota, it was still winter, the brown-grass, dirty-snow time of the year. It didn't matter because they had seen springtime in Oklahoma. A long trip had been made and the couple knew they had tried everything they could to start a family of their own. It is too bad that Indian women have to pay such a price to make an attempt with no guarantees. The operation was a success and they are waiting to see the results.

Having a family is not about making one anyway. So much of how a family works is out of our control. The way friends and family blend together, the way we rejoice when a baby is born, and the way we say good-bye when souls move on is a part of our culture that can't be changed by anyone. One of my first big stories in the Reservation newspaper was about the time a fire made a family out of everyone.

I had just arrived home after picking up my son, Jim, from work. We were standing in the kitchen talking before going to sleep. We both heard and felt the explosion. It was a loud but muffled sound. We looked in the direction of the noise. It was from the house next door.

"Oh no," my son said as he took off running toward the burning house. The flames were yellowish red and already as large as the house.

I called 911. While giving information to the dispatcher, I watched the flames grow larger. The kitchen clock said it was just after midnight. I got even more worried because my son was there while I was tied to the telephone. I hung up the phone as the flames continued to grow. I woke up my wife Patricia and told her what was happening.

I drove to the burning house. The front door was open and I could see inside the building. The stairs were on fire, the living room was burning and so was the kitchen. It was unnaturally bright in the yard. All the light came from the fire.

My son was near the back of the house. I saw Jackie, the mother, on the ground in front of the house. She was crying and moaning, "My babies, my babies." I saw Buddy, the father, running around in back of the house.

My son, Jim, said, "They're still in there, Dad."

I looked up at the bedroom window. Smoke and flames were coming out of the window. The window was broken in a jagged way where my son had tried to get inside the burning building.

We made a human ladder and my son climbed on my back to try to get into the bedroom. The flames were getting higher and hotter. From where I was standing, I could see the back stairs were on fire. Smoke and flames were coming out of the kitchen doors and windows. The heat was intense under the bedroom window. It was hotter up near the window where my son was trying to climb through the fire and smoke. The smoke was billowing in his face when I told him to get down. We thought of using a pickup truck parked in the yard to stand on to climb through the bedroom window. No one knew where the ignition keys were.

With the exception of the sounds of the burning, it

was quiet inside the house, no smoke alarms, nothing. Outside the house, Jackie was crying over and over, "My babies, my babies."

The flames were rapidly consuming the house. The bathroom window was now open and the smoke and flames were coming out of there. We tried the human ladder again but it was impossible to get near the window. The heat was too intense.

Paul and Calvin came running up. Paul, an older brother of the babies inside, tried to help. I sent our son, Calvin, to our house for water hoses. While he was gone, we tried to find something to prop against the house so we could try climbing in again. We couldn't find anything to use.

Calvin arrived with the hoses. Jim grabbed one and went to hook it up to the front faucet. I took the other hose and connected it to the rear faucet. I turned on the valve and nothing happened. No electricity, no water pressure. I unscrewed the hose in helpless frustration.

I could hear Jackie again. She was sobbing, still saying over and over, "My babies, my babies."

I looked around but couldn't see her. She had gone back into the burning building. We could hear her but didn't know where she was. We finally heard her in the basement utility room crying and searching for her babies.

It was hot and full of smoke as I went through the wood chute doorway and found her. I tried to get her to climb out but she wouldn't. I picked her up and carried her to the wood chute and pushed her outside. Patricia was there and she helped pull her out of the house, away from the smoke and flames.

Patricia held Jackie to keep her from going back into

the burning house. While cradling Jackie in her arms, Patricia listened to her cry, "My babies, my babies."

Both of us were holding her when Deputy Dennis Arnold of the Carlton County Sheriffs' Department arrived. We told him what we knew and he took charge of the scene. While he was walking behind the house, we told him we would need an ambulance for Jackie. Recognizing the danger posed by the propane tank, the deputy shut it off. He told us to push the pickup truck away from the house.

"Oh my God," the deputy's voice cracked. He sobbed when the full truth hit him.

We got between the house and the truck and pushed. The metal of the truck was too hot to touch with our bare skin. We used cloth-covered shoulders and pulled sleeves down over our hands to push the truck away.

Patricia was still holding Jackie when Calvin brought a blanket for her. The ambulance arrived and we carried Jackie to it. Her son, Paul, went with her to the hospital.

The first fire truck soon ran out of water. It carries fifteen hundred gallons but two hoses, each spraying one hundred gallons a minute, emptied the tank in about eight minutes. The firefighters stood empty-handed in frustration as the fire continued to consume the house.

Northrup Road was bumper to bumper with cars belonging to family and community members, the highway patrol, volunteer firefighters, and the just plain curious. The people watching stood at a respectful distance across the road as the tragedy unfolded. We were sad when we first realized the babies couldn't be saved. We looked for someone or something to blame. There was no one and nothing.

The highway patrolman said it was 1:20 when the second fire truck arrived. The hoses were connected and the firemen went back to fighting the fire—the fire that had already taken three young lives, Jeremiah, Jesse, and Dan. The hungry fire that almost took a few more.

We left the fire scene and picked up John, another brother of the babies, and took him to the hospital where everyone was gathering. The family—a Gramma, brothers, uncles, and cousins—were in the waiting room. Some cried and some hugged each other in their grief.

We came home and talked about the whole experience. We blamed ourselves for not doing more. It was a quick brutal fire that took the three babies. When I look out the window in that direction, now all I see is darkness.

The heat of a fire, like the warmth of a family, is hard to ignore and the pain caused by one can only be forgotten with the help of others. One night, I found out exactly how Jackie felt, crying for the life of her babies.

It was a normal evening. I was home from work and we had just finished supper when our son, Jim, came to the house. Earlier in the day we'd had an argument about his use of alcohol. I kicked him out of the house when he couldn't or wouldn't stop drinking. He resisted suggestions of an alcohol treatment program and seemed ashamed to talk with us.

When he came by, we offered him food but he refused. He didn't appear drunk and just went downstairs to his former bedroom. After a few minutes, I heard him come upstairs and go outside. Patricia and I were watching the evening news when I heard him call, "Dad."

I looked out in the front yard and didn't see him. I

looked out the side windows and didn't see him. I thought I was hearing things so I went back to watching the news.

"Dad," I heard again.

I went out the back door and saw him. He was standing in the backyard near the clothesline. He was facing the back door holding his rifle. He held it in front of himself, almost like the military position called "present arms." The death end of the barrel was stuck under his chin. His finger was on the trigger.

He looked up as I came out the back door. He said, "I'm ready to do it, Dad." He was standing about twenty feet away from me.

He closed his eyes and pulled the trigger. His head was thrown violently up and to one side. As I was running down the stairs, I was glad it was the .22 rifle and not the shotgun. As a combat veteran, I immediately had a flashback to other gunshots I have seen. I ran across the lawn to him. He was just starting to sag to the ground by the time I got there. I was functioning on two levels. One, I was back in Vietnam again. I quickly scanned the treeline looking for a sniper. I knew I wouldn't see one but had to look anyway. On the other level, I knocked the rifle from his hands and eased him down to the ground. I could tell he was still alive. The smell of gunpowder, the red blood on the green grass, plus the confused state of the victim added to the flashback I was having.

I went on automatic pilot. I could hear he was having trouble breathing. I rolled him around so his head was downhill, so the blood would drain out and not choke him. The entry wound was under his chin. It was bleeding but not too badly. I dreaded doing it but I knew I had to. I cautiously went through my son's hair, feeling for the exit wound. I couldn't find it. I felt through his hair again, couldn't find the exit wound.

Patricia came to the back door. I told her he had shot himself and to call an ambulance. While she was calling, I decided I could get him to the hospital more quickly since the ambulance had to come out then go back. She canceled the ambulance and told the dispatcher we were bringing him in. She brought a towel for the entry wound and held it there while I drove us all to town.

I broke a few traffic laws getting him to the hospital. The doctors and nurses took over after we got him inside the emergency room of the Cloquet, Minnesota, hospital. After being stabilized, he was transferred to the trauma center, thirty-five miles away. He would survive.

After two weeks, he was released from the hospital. The bullet had fractured his jaw. The .22 caliber round had lodged near his left ear. My son has had extensive counseling and treatment for alcohol abuse. On his road to recovery, he considers himself lucky for having survived the gunshot.

As for me, I still get a chill as I go out the back door. One question still baffles me. Why did he call me out to watch? I think he was really mad at me or knew I would be able to help. When I ask him about it, he just says, "I don't know."

Suicide is much more than statistics. It is also devastating for the family. My son was eighteen when he shot himself in the head. The suicide signals were ignored or overlooked by all of us. In retrospect, we should have noticed something was wrong when he cut his long hair and gave his clothes away. He never talked about it but I know he felt bad when his friend shot himself the year before. My son didn't know alcohol was a depressant. All he knew was that he felt rotten and wanted to drink.

Suicide is a deadly problem. Since my son's attempt, I have heard of two other young ones from this Reservation who shot themselves. One lived and the other died because he used a deer rifle.

Looking back in our history, it was the white man who brought guns and alcohol to our people. It would be silly to blame the white man for the way we use them.

When you were young, did you have a town drunk?

No, we all took turns.

They say alcohol has been used by generations of Shinnobs as a response to Reservation life. Who needs excuses? We need solutions so our children will quit killing themselves.

Families, like stories, go on. They have beginnings, endings, and you have to listen to understand them. Coming from a large, extended family means you have a lot of relatives. It also means you go to a lot of funerals.

Most recently, I was with my sister, Judy, when she died after a short illness. I was with her while waiting for the ambulance to take her to the hospital. The family members spent hour after hour with her during the death watch. She gradually got worse as her major organs shut down. Judy was sick from toxic shock syndrome, which had almost killed her two years earlier.

In those two years, Judy lived her life like she wanted.

She went to plays with friends. Judy cleaned rice through two seasons. Her children and grandchildren were always at her house, just visiting.

The doctors used morphine to ease her pain as she went from this world to the next. We had the wake and funeral in Sawyer. Friends and relatives gathered from all over Minnesota. Judy made a lot of friends in her time here on earth.

The feast after the graveside service was large. I counted six different wild rice dishes made by community women for the funeral feast. I thought it was fitting because Judy really liked to clean rice.

We live for our families. As I look around America, I see so many people who obviously don't have a feeling of family. I feel sorry for them as I continue my seasonal life on the Fond du Lac Reservation.

End of the Beginning

Someone said we begin to die
the minute we're born
Death is a part of life
Who knows why the Creator
thins his herd
Another old saying says
We must all be prepared
to give up those we love
or die first
Take time to mourn
take time to remember
Everything happens in cycles
The pain you feel was once
balanced by someone's joy

when that baby was born
The loss you feel today
will be replaced by good
long lasting memories
Is there a message here? Yah.
Treat others like this is your
last day above ground.

2
Seasons

....

Spring Summer
Fall Winter

ZIIGWANG NIIBING
DAGWAAGING BIBOONG

SEASONS ARE QUESTIONS and answers, patterns and surprises. Traditional Anishinaabeg life follows nature's changing cycles. From harvest to hibernation, sweet spring to summer wanderings. We know who we are from the seasons. When living with the seasons, we don't get worried about time as measured by the clock.

Nahgachiwahnong, now named the Fond du Lac Reservation, reflects the Creator's designs in silver birch, white pine, red oak, basswood, and tamarack trees. Sugar maple, blueberries, kinnikinnick, sage, and sweet grass are a few of the gifts. A sprinkling of lakes, small in comparison to nearby Lake Superior, offer enough wild rice to last from one season to the next.

Wild rice, manoomin in our language, is the annual autumn gift from the Creator. It appears at every celebration or sorrowful gathering. I make rice fanning baskets and harvest wild rice every year so this is where some of my stories start.

How could you tell she was a traditional Shinnob?

Her perfume was called Eau de Parched Rice.

According to the old stories, the Anishinaabeg would migrate west until they came to a place where food grows on the water. The Anishinaabeg lived near the wild rice before anyone arrived from Europe.

We make rice the way our parents and grandparents did. It just feels right to go out on the lakes to gather our share of the harvest. Ricing is hard work but we feel connected to the old days, the old ways when doing it.

Wild rice grows in the shallow lakes and rivers around the Reservation. The nutrient-rich mud at the bottom is where the rice germinates and takes root. All summer long we watch the plants grow. At first, it just breaks the surface of the water. After that, it lies on the water in the floating stage. The wild rice plants then stand up and grow, sometimes to a height of six feet above the water.

The rice plants flower and the rice grains ripen in late August and early September. The rice plants are a lighter shade of green than the balsam and pine trees that surround the water. The rice bed looks like a field of grass waving in the wind. The rice grains are near the top of the plant. It ripens near the top and the outer edges, then near the stalk. We can harvest rice day after day from the same plants as it ripens. The plants are treated with respect because it is a gift.

The tools used for making rice include a canoe, knockers, a pole, a large kettle, a dancing pit, and fanning baskets. In the old days, birch bark canoes were used to get out on the lake to harvest the rice. Today, our canoes are made from aluminum or canvas. We use carved cedar knockers to brush rice from the plants into the canoe. The knockers are made from a cedar log that has been quartered and then carved into a tapered shape. They are lightweight and become smooth from years of brushing the rice plants. The forked pole used to propel the canoe is made from two kinds of wood. I like to use spruce for the pole and diamond willow for the fork. Spruce because it is light and diamond willow because it is strong. My son, Jim, prefers wood with a twisted grain for the pole. Other Shinnobs like to use sumac for the fork.

The rice is harvested by two people in a canoe. The poler stands in front, propelling the canoe through the thick beds of wild rice plants. While standing, the poler can see where they are growing good and thick. It is the poler's responsibility to keep the knocker in the good rice. The knocker sits in the back, bending the plants over the canoe then stroking the heads to remove the ripe rice. The rice grains falling inside make a friendly sound as they hit the canoe bottom. The rice that falls into the lake is not wasted—it becomes next year's crop. The rice grains make a circular ripple, then dive to the bottom where they take root and grow. The barbed end, called the beard, keeps the grain at the right depth for germination.

We share the rice beds with the ducks, rice hens, muskrats, and others who depend on the Creator's gift. We always offer tobacco before we use any of the gifts of the Creator. We usually see eagles circling over us as we make rice. It is as if they are watching us make use of the gift.

After harvesting, we bring the rice home where we

spread it out to dry for a couple of hours. We turn it so it dries evenly. We also clean the plant stalks and leaves from the rice while it is drying.

We use our large parching kettle and a fire to further dry the rice. The black, three-legged cauldron is also called a treaty kettle. Our kettle has been handed down from family to family since treaty signing times in the nineteenth century.

The story that came with the kettle says it first came to the Anishinaabeg in Sandy Lake, a village west of our Reservation. Smallpox wiped out the village so the kettle came to Sawyer, our village. It lived with one family through many seasons of ricing and sugar bush. The son of the man who brought it to our village wanted to go to bingo one night so the kettle came to live with us.

It is propped up at an angle over the fire. We use dry birch and maple to fuel the flames. I like the way the wood smoke mixes with the rice during parching. I think it adds to the taste of the rice. When the heat is just right, we pour a basketful of rice into the empty kettle. The parcher uses a canoe paddle to stir the rice, turning it to keep it from burning.

At first, wisps of steam come off the green rice. The color gradually turns to brown as the stirring continues. The smell of parching rice is spread by the wind through the neighborhood. The odors of wood smoke and parching rice bring out family memories, generations old.

Deciding when to take the rice out of the kettle is an acquired skill. The color, the sound, and the way the rice moves help the parcher decide when the batch is done. Some Shinnobs prefer a hot, quick fire while others like a long, slow parch with a cooler flame.

We've heard that before treaty kettles, the Anishinaabeg used woven mats to parch the rice. They used a reed that doesn't burn to dry the rice over the fire.

The Anishinaabeg used different ways to remove the hulls from the grain. Two methods used a pit. In the old days, they were lined with deer or moose hides. Today, we line our pit with canvas. I tell my grandchildren that we have to remove the wrapper from the candy, remove the hulls from the grain.

One method used a rounded, wooden pole to pound the rice. Another way was to jig or dance on the rice. In this area we learned how to dance on the rice.

Patricia dances in our family. We were worried about making flour if I danced on it. She wears clean moccasins when dancing and leans on a pole suspended over the pit to take some of the weight off the rice. Patricia dances to music as she grinds the hulls off with her feet. Because we live in two worlds, the music comes from a powwow tape or a rock-and-roll radio station.

It usually takes a couple of times in the dancing pit before we get most of the hulls off. Next is fanning; we use our birch bark baskets to separate the hulls from the grains of rice.

Fanning with a basket makes me realize how essential the wind can be. I recognize the genius of the first people who designed the baskets. My family and I feel we are being close to the traditions when we make and use baskets like our elders did.

Fanners keep their backs to the wind while throwing rice in the air. The hulls are lighter than the grains and work their way to the top of the pile. The wind catches the hulls and blows them away from the basket. When there is no wind, the weight of the falling rice creates its own wind to blow the hulls out. The rice makes a familiar, distinct sound as it dances in the basket. Being able to bounce rice in the basket without losing it on the ground is also an acquired skill.

The final cleaning of the rice is a family affair. Everyone gets his or her turn at cleaning rice. We spend hours staring into the small world defined by the edge of a dinner plate. One by one the grains of rice that didn't lose their hulls are taken out. Slowly the pile of finished rice grows. It is mostly green in color. For us, cleaning rice at the kitchen table is best because of the sun coming through the windows. We go into winter knowing we have sacks of food. My gramma, Susan, kept her finished rice in pillowcases, many pillowcases in her closet. It seems like a natural place to keep my rice.

Now the rice can be stored for years. When we want to eat, it only takes eight minutes in boiling water.

Ricing is so central to our life that it could be as much a purpose as a privilege. It is true that we live with, and in some ways, for the rice.

Whenever Shinnobs meet on the road, at the bingo hall or clinic, the conversations always include ricing or stories about ricing. Some of the best ricing stories are retold during the season of making rice.

One of my favorites is the time some people sold a rice buyer something other than wild rice. They added a couple of big rocks to increase the weight of the rice sacks. The next day, the rice buyer came back and sold the people some groceries. The people found the same rocks in their flour. Like most stories, this one could be five minutes or five hours long depending on the skill of the storyteller. The story apparently really happened in the 1930s or '40s.

The power of the story comes from our reaction to it.

One person could hear it and reaffirm their belief that cheaters never prosper. Another could listen to the same story and say, "Well, we tried that trick on the white man and it didn't work. We'll have to come up with a better one than that."

A third could hear nothing beyond the fact that it was a ricing story. They could take a little trip back to the last time they were ricing. The memories would bring smiles.

Someone else might say, "Hey, wait a minute, he just stole my best story about rocks and rice."

A businessman might say, "What the hay, the guy still made money. The rocks were more valuable as rice than as flour."

"I remember my Dad telling this story," would be another response as yet another listener traveled back in family history to an image of her Dad laughing, as he told the same story.

I listen to and tell ricing stories.

Some stories are about people who are not ready for ricing. I met a woman who said she was going to attend a four-day workshop on wild rice. The seminar was to take place in Ely, a canoe town in northern Minnesota. She gushed about the workshop like it was one of those mystical Boundary Waters Canoe Area Wilderness experiences. The first day would be spent making knockers and a pole. The rest of the four days would be spent harvesting, parching, dancing, and fanning, then eating the product of their labors. She didn't indicate if she would get continuing education credits for the wild rice project. As an interested ricer, I asked what she would do to get the rice beards out of her eye. She said, "What are rice beards?"

She'll find out soon enough when she gets out on the

lake and discovers that rice beards stick to everything, including the eyes and mouth. I just can't picture wild rice as a "project."

How could you tell she was a rookie ricer?

She was using a kayak.

Each year, the Minnesota Department of Natural Resources makes an official announcement about the opening of the wild rice season. Some of us suspect a dart and a calendar are used to select the date. Wild rice may be ripe in the southern part of the state but only flowering in the northern part. People who don't know or respect the gift go out and pound on the rice. The premature harvesting damages the growing plants. On my Rez, a rice committee sets the opening date for each lake.

As these preparations are taking place, the highway becomes littered with white vendors selling their black paddy rice product. They even dare to call it wild rice. The vendors fool the tourists all summer with their cheap, manufactured product that is anything but wild.

We know a lot of paddy rice is grown in California where it is sprayed with chemicals and harvested mechanically. Friends tell me it takes a long time to cook the paddy rice product. Some say soaking it overnight helps. Others report boiling it hour after hour. After hearing about it, I suggested a recipe. First, find a baseball-sized rock. Add that to the water/paddy rice mixture that is boiling. Cook until the rock is soft; that means your rice is almost done. I have never knowingly tasted that paddy rice product and I could die happy without doing it.

Wild rice season means different things to different people. In my family, we pass through July and August telling stories and making baskets while waiting for the Creator's gift. A Northrup specialty, the sturdy, shallow fanning baskets are born during the heat that precedes the harvest. The design is copied from my Grampa's baskets.

There is no shopping mall that I know of that sells birch bark or fanning baskets. We go to the woods to gather the materials, just like the Shinnobs before us.

Does it hurt the tree when you remove the bark?

No. Do you live in a wood house or read a news-paper?

All trees look good from a distance. The white birch is easy to see in the green, green of the surrounding woods. The search for the right piece of bark takes you deeper and deeper into the woods. For some Shinnobs of this land, going to the woods just feels right. Sort of like going to a church, a mosque, a temple, a shrine, and a rummage sale all at the same time.

Selecting the right piece of bark requires a lot of walking and looking. We choose bark that is smooth with small black lines. We thank the Creator for the use of the bark by leaving an offering of tobacco.

A shallow cut is made into the selected tree. We never go too deep; the tree will die if the orange, inner layer is damaged. There is a popping, cracking sound as the bark comes off the tree. The wet, inner bark feels smooth on the fingertips.

The birch bark is unique. The best bark for our use is General Custer yellow, as we call it. There are marks where branches once grew. Some of the marks look like birds in flight. Around here, the bark peels easily for just a short time in June and July. I have noticed the bark peels well when the deerflies first start biting.

The three parts of the basket grow close to one another. While gathering birch, we also gather basswood bark for the stitching and green willow for the frames. This would be the Shinnob version of a stop at the Mall of America.

We must prepare the materials before we use them. We use the outer layer of the birch and the inner layer of the basswood bark. The frames must be bent, tied, and dried.

It takes about twelve hours to make one basket. Making baskets is a mellowing experience. We can't work on them when angry or in a hurry. The fragile materials will not cooperate if treated roughly. We take pride in finishing a basket. If they are treated like a gift from the Creator, they will last forty years or longer.

Some of our baskets are hanging in museums in Minnesota. Of course, a lot of them are used every ricing season here on the Rez. We demonstrated how we make baskets in New York City at The National Museum of the American Indian. But more important, a family member compared ours to the ones my Grampa used to make.

We like to teach what we have learned about making baskets. Ezigaa learns one more thing each year about birch bark basket making. Learning leads to teaching. Like using the language, basket making and ricing keep our culture alive.

It is not enough to know something; to really make it a part of your life, you need to share it with friends and future generations. I feel sorry for all the Shinnobs who know it is ricing time but can't get out on the lakes. The constraints of jobs, kids, school walls, jail bars, and health keep them from taking part in the annual harvest. I think I would be out of sync all year if I couldn't make rice.

I taught my son, Joseph, about wild rice. It was his first time on the lake as a ricer, a Rez rite of passage. I started off by showing him how to pole the canoe through the rice. I could almost hear him saying, "Wait, let me see if I got this right. Stand up in front of the canoe? Okay, then push against the plants with this long, skinny pole? Wait, let's go back to that standing up in the canoe part."

He was a bit awkward at first but his natural athletic ability helped. At one point when we first started off, he wanted to quit. We were out on the lake so he couldn't walk off the job. Eventually he got the hang of it and was smiling as he moved the canoe through the rice.

After he felt good about moving the canoe, I let him try knocking the rice. He was tentative at first but did show potential as an all-around ricer. He came to understand that there is a lot more to rice than just eating it. We brought the rice home and I showed him how I like to parch. He needed help at first but soon learned what to look and listen for when parching rice. After dancing and fanning, we had twenty pounds of finished rice. As a proud parent, I let him have the day's harvest. More important, he will have something to teach his children.

After you parch the rice,
how long does it stay green?

Until I eat it, then it turns brown.

Some years are good and some bad as the Creator balances things out. One year we tried our usual spots and couldn't find a good lake to set our canoe in. The Rez lakes were especially poor, hardly enough for a skinny family of ducks, as my cousin, Chuck Greensky, said.

The Shinnobs of East Lake, a village west of our Rez, invited Sawyer ricers to come visit and rice on their lake. The community members showed one of the strong cultural traits of the Anishinaabeg—generosity. They could have kept their lake closed but did not. Instead, they were sharing. I think the Sawyer ricers will remember that act of kindness for a few generations.

Ezigaa and I were standing on the lakeshore one fine ricing morning. It was cool but the bright sun was warming things up nicely. The overnight dew was leaving the plants. We were watching my two sons, Jim and Joseph. They were using my canoe to go out and harvest rice. I got profound when I realized I had seen four generations of Anishinaabeg harvesting rice. I decided to give my grandson a quiz.

"Ezigaa, who made that rice?"

"The Creator," he answered.

"What about the water, who made the water?"

"The Creator," the four-year-old boy said.

"How about those ducks, who made them?"

"The Creator," he said.

"Who made Ezigaa?" I asked.

"The Creator."

I thought my grandson had been paying attention. I was not prepared some time later when he asked, "Grampa, who made the Creator?"

I think of ricers who once lived and now only exist in stories. I remember who riced with whom. I know who showed me the difference between lakes. Some lakes are known for having long grains of rice while other lakes have short, fat grains. Over the years, the ricers have learned which rivers ripen first, which lake ripens last.

Ricing ends each year with memories like these. Every part of ricing connects me with my food, my family memories, and the seasons.

We feel prepared for winter with pillowcases of green wild rice. The leaves begin to turn as winter approaches. I like the way a friend described it. Gert Morris, an elder from Cass Lake, said, "The weather is painting all the trees."

As the days get shorter and the nights get longer, we stay inside more. We take the usual precaution of dressing in layers—many, many layers to survive the northern Minnesota winters. I tell my grandson stories of how my Grampa used to sleep outside when it was 30 below with just a blanket when he was trapping. He built a bed of balsam and slept with his feet to the fire.

When I was young we didn't have windchill. Somebody would say, "Cold."

"Windy too," someone would answer.

Today, thanks to those weather fluffs on TV, I can tell you it is precisely 32 below zero with a windchill of 74 below. I was watching their part of the evening news when I heard one of them, with all sincerity, say, "Last night was the coldest night ever." As if we didn't have weather before the white man came and started keeping track. The cultural arrogance of that young white pup, I thought. Now does that white man think they invented weather? I know from the old stories it was colder here when the glacial ice was a mile thick.

In spite of the cold, we still have to get around. It is an annual challenge to keep our cars running in the winter.

The Rez gets littered with winter-kill cars. There is something about 30 below that tests the metal of the car and the mettle of the driver. Everyone who drives has a dead car story. Plastic antifreeze jugs of various colors accumulate. Most people have electric engine block heaters to keep their cars warm. Even so, some folks still go out and start their cars every two hours to make sure they will run during the really cold spells.

Over the years I have learned to carry certain supplies in a winter emergency kit. I need: gas line antifreeze, radiator antifreeze, starting fluid, jumper cables, a battery charger, a tow chain, a shovel, a ten-pound bag of paddy rice for traction, and a ten-pound box of twenty-dollar bills.

Do you get much snow on the Rez?

Well, it's ass deep to a tall Shinnob.

I am glad to see the occasional snowstorm. When it falls, it covers up the old, used-up snow. I used to think snow only came in one color. As an adult, I look around and see all the different colors. I see brown snow where it has been salted and sanded. I see the almost blue of fresh new snow and the gray of snow at dusk. I like the diamonds that sparkle when the sun hits the snow just right. I am glad we have changing seasons so I can recharge in winter. This is the storytelling time of the year.

Here's one that might explain why Shinnobs are known among other tribes as "rabbit chokers." The story is written first in English and then Ojibwe. When using the Ojibwe, I have two goals. The first is to preserve the language by using it. The second is to show how expressive, how complex the language can be. The translation from English to Ojibwe is provided by Neeb, David Aubid, an Ojibwe language teacher who keeps me from mixing verb tenses in two languages. To help catch the flow of the story, I will provide selected English equivalents after the Ojibwe version. Please note that the transliteration of Ojibwe words is inexact when various English tenses are involved, so bear with me if you notice some inconsistent spellings.

Winter was here and my grandson and I went out in the woods to see if we could choke some rabbits. We were tired of TV.

Biboon. Ninoozhishenh miinawaa gayeniin nin-dizhaamin iwidi megwayaak nandawaabamangwaa waaboozoog genagwaanindwaa. Mii onji i'iw azaam apane ninganawaabandaamiin i'iw mezinaateseg.

Biboon	Winter
Ninoozhishenh	My grandson
miinawaa	and, also, again

iwidi	over there
megwayaak	in the woods
waaboozoog	rabbits
Mii	it is thus that
onji	for a certain reason
apane	always, all the time, continually
i'iw	that
mezinaateseg	television

Snaring is an old and honorable profession among the Shinnobs of northern Minnesota. I told my wife that this is the time of the year when Shinnobs check their trap lines. She shook her Dakota head and said, "A one-snare trap line?" (Trappers usually set many, many traps.)

I'iw nagwaaganewin mewinzha ogii-kikendaa-nawaa onizhishinining ingiw Ojibwe Anishinaabeg omaa gaa ayaajig omaa noongom ezhinikaadeg Min-isodakiing. Ningii-wiidamawaa niwiiw mii apii neyaaji-wanii'igewaad ingiw Anishinaabeg. Wewe-bikenid a'aw Bwaanikwe, mii dash ezhi-madwe ikidod, "Mii i'iw bezhig nagwaagan aawang onaaji-wanii'igewin ina?"

nagwaaganewin	snaring
mewinzha	a long time ago, long ago
ingiw	those
omaa	here
noongom	now, today, nowadays
Minisodakiing	Minnesota
niwiiw	my wife

apii	when, then, at the time
Bwaanikwe	Dakota woman
ikidod	said
bezhig	one
nagwaagan	snare

We're already starting to hear Sawyer Shinnob snaring stories. One guy said he got one rabbit and an owl got the other. The owl did leave the empty snare and certain internal parts. We went out in the woods to snare our own stories.

Mii gaabige noondamaang ingiw Gwaaba'iganii-Anishinaabeg odibaajimowiniwann gayewiina-waa gii-agoodamawaawaad iniw waaboozoon. Bezhig inini dabibaajimod; bezhig waaboozoon gii-ayaawaad miinawaa gayewiin a'aw gookooko'oo bezhig waaboozoon gii-ayaawaad. A'aw gookooko'oo ogii-nagadaanan i'iw bezhishigwaag nagwaagan miinawaa aanind a'aw waabooz onaagizhiin. Megwaayaak ningii-izhaamin ji gagwe nagwaadamaang gayeniinawind ge-ni-dibaadodamaang.

noondamaang	hearing
Gwaaba'iganii-Anishinaabeg	Sawyer Shinnob
iniw	those
inini	man
gookooko'oo	owl

Ezigaa was about to join the ranks of rabbit chokers. He has been on the planet for almost five years and has never set a snare. His education was lacking until today.

Ezigaa mii azhigwa de-apiitizid ji wiijiiwaad ingiw negwaajigejig. Mii naano-biboon abiitang gayewiin oo'o aki, gaawiin idash mishi agoojigesiin. Ogikendaasowin o'o keyaa ji maajiishkaamagadinig azhigwaa.

Ezigaa	Wood tick
azhigwa	now, at this time, already
wiijiiwaad	go with someone, accompany someone
naano-biboon	be five years
aki	earth, land, ground, country
gaawiin	no, never
agoojigesiin	hang things
maajiishkaamag- adinig	start to move
Ogikendaasowin	his education

We began by studying the tracks. Ezigaa learned the difference between rabbit and dog tracks. He could also tell which tracks were new and which were old. While looking at the tracks, Ezigaa showed me how the rabbits leave those marks. He crouched down and did a fair imitation of a rabbit hopping through the snow.

Ingii-maajitaamiin, ganawaabandamaang anooj awesiinhyag ezhi-bimikawewaad. Ezigaa ogii-gikendaanan keyaa ezhi-bakaanakin iniw obimi-

kawaaganiwaana'aw animosh miinawaa a'aw waa-
booz. Miinawaa ogii-nasidawinaanan wenji-
bakaaninaagwak iniw gete-bimikawaaganan
miinawaa iniw oshki-bimakawaaganan. Megwaa
ganawaabandang a'aw waabooz obimikawaa-
ganan; Ezigaa niwaabanda'ig naabinootawaad
keyaa ezhi-inenimaad iniw waaboozon ezhichigenid
apii gaa-ozhüttoogwen iniw obimikawaaganan apii
gaa-gwasshkwanid imaa gooning.

anooj	various, all kinds
awesüinhyag	wild animals
ezhi	in a certain way, to a certain place, thus
bimikawaan	footprint, track
gikendaanan	know something
animosh	dog
gete-bimikawaa-ganan	old tracks
oshki-bimikjawaa-ganan	new tracks
megwaa	while, during
a'aw	that
naabinootawaad	repeat what someone says, mock someone
inenimaad	think of someone a certain way
gaa	a past tense prefix
ozhitoogwen	make something, build something, form something
gwasshkwanid	jump
imaa	there
gooning	snow

Just being in the woods with the little boy brought back memories. First, of course, was the cold. It was 10 below and felt like 50 below. We were layered up so the cold was no problem. Then there was the snow. My grandson is tall enough now to walk in the woods without tripping all the time. It makes it easier. I could see he was learning how to walk through the brush and snow. I remembered walking behind as Grampa or some older relative broke trail for me. I felt good to be breaking trail for my grandson.

Megwaa wiijiiwag wa'wa gwiiwizens babaa-ayaayaang megwayaakong ningii-gezikwendaan anooj gegoo. Ninitami-mikwenjigan mii iw gaa-apiichi ginsinaag. Noongom idash gaye wenda-gisinaa; niiskaadad. Mii de minik gaa-biizikamaang, ningii-zhoozimin. Mii miinawaa i'iw bezhig mekwen-damaan i'iw isa gii-koonikaag. Ninoozhishenh mii zhigwa de iniginid weweni ji babaamosed meg-wayaakong. Apane ko' gii-pizozideshing, nawaj noongom wenipanizi. Noongom mikwenimag keyaa gaa-izhi-gikendang ji ni nitaabimosed imaa gii-koonikaanig megwekobing. Niingii-kezikwenimaag ingiw gaa-noopinanagwaa gayewiinawaa ozhi-toowaapan omiikanensiwaan imaa gii-koonikaag. Ningii-jiikendam gikendamaan azhigwaa gayeniin noopinanid ninoozshishenh.

wiijiiwag	go with someone, accompany someone
gwiiwizens	boy
gezikwendaan	vaguely remember something

gegoo	something
wenda	really, completely, just so
gisinaa	be cold (weather)
niiskaadad	be bad weather
weweni	properly, correctly, carefully
babaamosed	walk about
wenipanizi	be easy
nitaa	know how to do something, being good at

We waded through the snow until we began seeing rabbit tracks. I showed Ezigaa how I like to hang a snare. We picked a rabbit freeway.

Imbabaamosemin imaa ishpaagonagaag, baa-maa igo waabandamaang waaboozoog obimika-waaganiwaan. Ezigaa niwaabanda'aa keyaa niin ezhi-minwendamaan agoodawag a'aw waabooz. Waaboozo gichi-mikana ningii-onaabandaamin.

imaa	there
baamaa	later
igo	emphatic word
niin	I, me
ezhi	thus, so, there, in a certain way
minwendan	like something
agoodawag	set a snare for someone
a'aw	that
gichi	big, great, very
miikana	road, trail

The snare is made from picture hanging wire. It has a noose fashioned at one end. The other end is wrapped around a heavy stick, heavy enough so the rabbit can't drag it home.

Nagwaagan ozhichigaadeg aabajichigaademagad i'iw biiwaabiko biiminakwaanens (agoojigaadeg mazinaakizowinan). Wawawiiyechigaademagad we-weni waabooz oshtigwaaning ji zhaabosenig ji ni minokang, ji naabikawaaganid. I'iw biiwaaiko bi-iminakwaanens eyaaman, aazhiwayiyiing keyaa imaa gaa-ozhitooyan onaabikawaagan, mii iwidi awas keyaa ji ni aabajitooyan ji ni dadibiiginaman imaa mitigoonsing: a'aw mitigoons weweni gaa-onaambamad ge-bwaaninang a'aw waabooz ji gin-jiba' iwebaatoosig.

nagwaagan	snare
ozhchigaade	be made, be built
aabajichigan	tool
biiwaabik	metal, iron
biiminakwaan	rope
agoojige	hang things
zhaabose	go through, pass through
minokan	fit something well
mitigoons	stick, piece of wood
ginjiba'	flee from someone

We used dry branches from the nearest balsam tree to close the exits on the rabbit freeway. Ezigaa caught on right away to what I was doing. He helped build the fence that would channel the rabbits through the snare. The snare was set.

Iniw gaa-nibomagakin wadikwanan imaa zhin-gobiing ningii-pakwaajibidoomin, gii-ni shezhegosi-dooyaang jiigi-nawaaganing imaa gaa-agoodeg nasawai'iing owaaboozo gichi miikaniwaa. Mii gwayak imaa da apatoowag ogii-enendaanaadog gayewiin Ezigaa, gayewiin isa gii-wiidookaazod. Mii gakina gegoo gii-kiizhising.

zhingob	balsam fir
gwayak	straight, right, correct
apatoo	run to a certain place, run in a certain way
wiidookaazo	help
gakina	all
gegoo	something

Then the hard part came. We ran around in the woods trying to chase a rabbit through the snare.

Mii omaa dash apii gichi-zanagak. Ningii-babaamibatoomin megweyaakong, waaboozoog gagwe-izhinaazhikawindwaa iwidi agoojiganing.

dash	and
zanagizi	be difficult
babaamibatoo	run about
megwaayaak	in the woods
gagwe	try

Naw, I was just kidding about that part. Instead, we went home and warmed up.

Anisha gosha. Gego debwetangen! Ningii-kiiwe-min; gii awazoyaang, gosha.

Anisha	just for nothing, just for fun, not really
gego	don't
debwe	tell the truth
awazo	warm oneself by the fire

My grandson asks every morning if it is time to check the snare. I think he likes the walk in the woods with his Grandpa. I can hardly wait to see the look on his face when we actually catch a rabbit. Another rabbit choker is born.

Endaso-gigizhebaawagak ninoozhishenh imbi-gagwejimig mii apii ge naaji-nagwaaganeyang mi-inawaa na? Aapiji nimisawendaan ji waabamag ge inidengwed apii geget bezhig waabooz naagwaa-nang. Mii miinawaa bezhig waboozo-gibinewewinini gii ondaadizid.

endaso	every, so many
gigizhebaawagak	morning
na	(yes/no question word)
Aapiji	very, quite
waabam	see someone
geget	sure, indeed, certainly, really
gibinewen	choke someone
ondaadizi	be born

If that Energizer Bunny ever comes around here. . . .

Giishpin a'aw inigaazid waabooz babaa-ayaad omaa. . . .

Giishpin	if
inigaazi	be poor, be pitiable
babaa	going about

For many of us now, especially the younger ones, the approach of winter only means one thing—school. My experience with learning ranges from time in the woods, where I have found school unnecessary; to my own memories of boarding schools, federal and Christian; to the schools we have now where my children and grandchildren spend long days. I occasionally visit schools to broaden America's view of us.

On one of my trips into the world of American education, I was headed to Southwest State University in Marshall, Minnesota. Due to a misread schedule, I arrived five minutes and twenty-four hours early. Once I found out, I tried to pretend it was all planned that way. Since Pipestone, Minnesota, was just forty miles away, I decided to go there and look around.

It's been decades since I was a student at Pipestone Boarding School. I looked for the familiar buildings that I had seen as a six-year-old Shinnob in the late 1940s. All I saw was the gym, the superintendent's house, and the hospital. The school building, the boys' dormitory, the girls' dormitory were all gone. The old Sioux quartzite buildings had been torn down to make room for a technical college. Part of the grounds were being used for a nursing home. I remembered the two stone pillars by the road to town.

After looking around for a while, I drove to town. I found the Pipestone County Museum and toured the exhibits. Of course, they had pipestone on display.

I met Joe Ager, the director of the museum. He

showed me a collection of photographs taken when the boarding school was in operation. The buildings in the photos were sure familiar. In one picture of the boys' dormitory, I found the window out of which I would look for home, three hundred miles away. It was the third window from the northeast corner of the big red building.

Joe told me the white farmers around Pipestone were paid a bounty for reporting runaway Indians. He told me the white townsfolk would like to forget that part of their town's history.

While looking at the photographs, I wondered, had anyone collected a bounty on me when I ran away from the school? I left the museum and went back to the school grounds. The ever-blowing wind was familiar as was the black soil of the surrounding corn fields.

It made me sad to be there, a long time kind of sad. I remembered the lonesome nights again.

I escaped like I did when I was young. I strolled down the sidewalk where the girls' dormitory used to be. I casually stepped behind the superintendent's house and sprinted for the brush.

I walked to the waterfall located in the national park. I just sat there, soaking up the positive ions from the moving water. The sound was relaxing and I forgot about the crying and the boys' dormitory. While there, I found the local landmark, the Great Stone Face. I looked at it, then went behind and jumped out to the top of it. The leap across wasn't as scary as when I was young.

Being in that place reminded me how much I have survived. Not just me, but all the lonely, homesick Shinnobs who went to Pipestone Boarding School.

I picked up a couple of pieces of Sioux quartzite. They looked like parts of the old buildings. I brought the rocks home to cousins and friends who, like the overlooked rocks, had survived the boarding school experience.

Today, our children live at home while attending school. They find that old American attitudes about us still linger. In 1991, a professor from a university in Duluth, Minnesota, surveyed some fourth- and fifth-grade students about their impressions of us. The survey took place in Bloomington, Minnesota. Judge their answers yourself and imagine my reaction.

- They could be like us if they worked hard.
- If I saw an Indian, I'd be scared stiff.
- They always attacked pilgrims.
- The Indians were mean.
- No one can say Indians aren't people.
- They all eat raw meat.
- Whenever they killed a cowboy, they scalped him.
- Indians mean big trouble.
- Indians fought to save their land.
- They killed white men.
- The big chiefs would jump over four feet of fire.
- They tell lies and fibs.
- They have funny names.
- They had very weird customs.
- I think Indians are brave.
- People think there is something wrong with Indians, that's why they have Reservations.
- When the teacher told us they were still alive, it sure surprised me.
- They were the first people here but did not discover America.

- They're dumb, they believe in spirits.
- I don't mind them if I'm not by them.
- They are afraid of whites because of our sickness.
- They are lazy.
- They are fat.
- On TV, they are messy and kill a lot.
- They were real boozers.
- They'll be nice if we are.
- Friendly, if you don't hurt them.
- I like Indians.
- They are wig collectors.
- They are fun to visit in camp.
- They still live in teepees, are hungry, and probably have no clothes.
- There aren't many in my city.
- They dug into a child's skin as punishment.
- They wore war paint.
- They liked firewater.
- They all have red skin and dark hair.
- They have so many mothers, they don't know which one is theirs.
- They don't hunt for fun.
- They were the first Americans.
- They gave us names.
- They have long hair.
- Their doctors are dumb.
- They live in the Black Hills.
- Sometimes they had wars and many people were injured.
- Now there are too many white people to kill so they live on Reservations.
- They believe there is a spirit god but there really isn't.
- They are neglected.

The survey results would be funny if they weren't so sad, sad if they weren't so funny. Why are there so many responses in the past tense? Only one lonely, "I like Indians" amidst so much fear. Naming, wars, and differences leap out. It shows that after five hundred years and two thousand seasons, most American children still don't know us. Whose fault is it anyway? What, if anything, can we do to help the people still teaching such nonsense at home or school?

I'm not sure if we can change all those little minds. I am busy each year visiting schools of white children and magnet schools for Shinnobs. I try to spread the stories of the Anishinaabeg.

Some schools, like Four Winds in Minneapolis, are keeping the language alive. When I visited that school, the students sang "Twinkle, Twinkle, Little Star," in Ojibwemowin, the formal name for our language. Some parts of childhood translate across cultures beautifully. At the Heart of the Earth Survival School in Minneapolis, they have circle time each week. The students are released from the classrooms to attend pipe ceremonies and to sing and dance. Two traditional drums mark time for the songs. The young singers follow the lead of an older man who teaches them the songs. Young dancers practice in the background. Squirmy second graders watch the pipe ceremony. The smell of sage is everywhere. The dancers show "happy feet," as my brother, Jeff, calls it. The students move through the school as if they own it, welcoming people to their place.

Some schools are all lessons while others offer circle time and language instruction. The best for Anishinaabeg children include Ojibwemowin.

Indians have been removed from their homes and

families. When I was young, it was boarding schools. Today it is foster homes and other social service agencies that separate us. This brings frustration, which can lead to substance abuse of alcohol and other drugs. It also leads to adults who have no parenting skills, to adults who are lost children.

Long ago, we didn't send our children to another tribe to raise; we did it ourselves. Just as we are asked to share our history with other people, we need to remember to pass it on to our own children. Anishinaabeg children should know their own history and language along with their ancestors' contributions to the present. In the Great Lakes area, just learning the language teaches all children about the presence of the Anishinaabeg.

How do you say moose in Ojibwe?

Mooz.

How do you say moccasin in Ojibwe?

Makizin.

Some things can't be improved.

When I was a young boy in boarding schools, the use of Ojibwe was discouraged. We had Ojibwe pounded out of us and English pounded in. It was the accepted social policy at the time.

Friends who could speak Ojibwe fluently made fun of us because we couldn't speak or understand the language when we came home from boarding school. I couldn't answer because I was too busy learning English. Somewhere along the way, I started to feel the impact of my loss. I no longer understood what the elders were saying. I especially hated it when I knew they were talking about me. There were times when it seemed like the older generations were ashamed of speaking it. They never used it when white people were around. For the most part, there was no effort made to teach the language. Sadly, Ojibwe went underground and stayed there for a long time.

Poet Adrian Louis said something like, "Respect your elders? They're the ones who got us in this mess." At times, I felt that way about Ojibwe language speakers. Most of us learned a few phrases because we were around Ojibwe speakers. We learned a little but not enough. We mostly learned the command words: don't, be quiet, sit down, don't cry, eat, or go to bed. It is hard to carry on a conversation using only command words.

A cousin said for the first eight years of his life, he thought his name was Gego, the Ojibwe word for don't.

Now there is a renewed interest in the Ojibwe language. Most colleges around here have classes that teach the language. Head Start programs and elementary schools on the Reservation encourage the use of Ojibwe. There are language tapes available now. I have seen Ojibwe language pages on the world wide web.

I agree that this is a good idea but am bitter that I had to wait forty years for it to happen. I use a language tape when I take long road trips in the car. My vocabulary is getting larger and I have more tools to express myself. I like to say I am fluent in Ojibwe but my vocabulary is extremely limited. With resources like my elders, tapes, and books like the University of Minnesota

Press's *Concise Dictionary of Minnesota Ojibwe,* I can continue to learn.

I have found the part of winter that is hard to ignore is Christmas. What a bummer.

My earliest memories of Christmas were formed at the federal boarding school. We were given presents of ribbon candy and fruit. All it meant to me was some big guy was going to beat me up and take my presents. Later, in the Christian boarding school, I was older so no one beat me up but Christmas was still a disappointment. It was about that time I learned that there is no such thing as goodwill towards men.

What does a Shinnob Santa say?

Ho, ho, ho-wah.

In Vietnam, Bob Hope came to help us celebrate the holiday. I couldn't figure out the link between peace on earth and a rice paddy firefight.

When my oldest son, Jim, was in the first grade, he told the teacher we don't celebrate Christmas. She went out of her way and bought him a fake tree. We thanked her but left it in the box and later gave it to someone who does celebrate Christmas.

Today there is no tree in my house. We just leave them outside where they continue to grow. No tinsel, angels, stars, or cute manger scenes. My electric bill stays the same because we don't outline the house in colored lights. I could never make the connection between colored lights and the birth of the Christ child. The only real connection I can make is that power companies sponsor lighting contests every year. I don't know how they judge these contests. Is it artistic quality or the total amount of electricity consumed?

No frenzied shopping at the mall for us. When we want to give a gift, we just do it regardless of the season. It is a year-round activity for us, but we usually wait until after Christmas when the prices come down in the clearance sales.

I am proud to be called Scrooge but I am not the Grinch that stole Christmas. I just ignore it and it goes away on its own. I am still confused about who we should be honoring at this time of the year—Santa Claus or Christ?

Then there is Easter. I'm having a hard time understanding that one. I grew up hearing about the Christian reason for the holiday. The way it is celebrated now confuses me.

Let me see if I have this straight. It all begins with a pre-Easter sale in the retail stores. An unusual rabbit lays and delivers pastel-colored chicken eggs. The *Waabooz* also lays chocolate eggs. The gender of this strange critter is never mentioned. Green plastic grass is part of it somewhere. The kids are teased by hiding the food. They look for and collect the bunny's leavings. Each year the pastel-colored eggs are rolled down the White House lawn. Everyone gets new clothes and the ladies get a bonnet to wear in the Easter parade. The doings are concluded with an after-Easter sale in the retail stores. I wish the Easter Bunny would come hop-hopping by my Rez, I can use the snare left over from the Energizer Bunny.

Meanwhile the seasons roll on regardless of the sales in the retail stores.

We are tapping maple trees as we do every year. As I travel around Indian country, I see more and more Indian people going to the sugar bush.

Niinawind, niiwii-ozhiga'igawaanaanig ingiw in-inaatigoog, mii ezhichigeyaang endaso-ziigwang. Babaa-izhaayaan Anishinaabeg odenawitoowaad, niwaabamaag eshkam nawaj niibowa Anishinaabeg izhaawaad iwidi iskigamizigaaning.

Niinawind	we
ininaatigoog	maples
endaso	every
ziigwang	spring
niwaabamaag	I see
eshkam	gradually, more and more
nawaj	more
niibowa	many, much
izhaa	go to a certain place
iwidi	over there
iskigamizigan	sugar bush

The crows tell us when it is time for making maple syrup. Two bald eagles flew over the fire when we were boiling the water out of the sap.

Mii ingiw aandegwag bebi-dibaajimojig apii ji ni maajitaang wii-ozhitoong zhiiwaagamizigan. Niizh migiziwag gii-pabaamisewag giiwitaayayi'iing imaa nindishkodeminaan megwaa iskigamizigeyaang

ingiw	those
aandegwag	crows
dibaajimo	tell, narrate
maajitaa	start an activity
ozhitoon	make something, build something
zhiiwaagamizigan	syrup
niizh	two
migiziwag	bald eagles
megwaa	while, during
iskigamizige	boil things down (e.g. maple sap)

We have a small sugar bush, barely over one hundred taps. We take only what we need for feast and funerals, gifts and pancakes.

Agaasaamagad nindiskigamiziganinaan; bangii awashime ingodwaak ozhiga'iganan. Mii eta minik memooyaang ge-aabajitooyaang ani ashangeng miinawaa apii awiiya ishkwaa-ayaad wiisining miinawaa imaa ningwekiwebiniganinaanin.

agaasaa	be small
bangii	a little, a little bit, few
awashime	much more
ingodwaak	one hundred
ozhiga'ige	tap trees
mii	it is thus that, it is that
eta	only
ashange	feed people, serve food to people
awiiya	somebody, anybody

Once again it was a learning experience for our grandchildren. They helped us gather sap from the trees. They are too young to help with the boiling so they just watched and listened when we told sugar bush stories.

Mii go miinawaa ji gikinawabiwaad ninoozhishe-hyag. Wiidookaazowag naadoobiiwaad. Gaawiin de apiitizisiiwag ji wiidookaagewaapan imaa iskigam-izigaadeg i'iw ziinzibaakwadaaboo, mii dash eta bizindamowaad keyaa ezhi-dadibaajimoyaang gaa-izhiwebak gii-iskigamizigeng.

mii	it is thus that, it is that
gikinawaabi	learn by observation
wiidookaazo	help
naadoobiiwaad	go get water or other liquid, gather sap
apiitizi	be a certain age
iskigamizige	boil things down (e.g. maple sap)
ziinzibaakwa-daaboo	maple sap
gaa	past tense prefix
izhiwebak	happen a certain way

We watched winter turn into spring. The sun was warm and reminded us of summer. The wind was cold and a reminder of the winter that just left.

Ningii-Kanawaabandaamin ani iskwaa-biboong ani-ziigwang idash. A'aw giizis wenda aabawaa-chige mii dash iw wenji-mikwendamaang gii-niibing.

*Dakaasin: mii miinawaa mikwendaagwak noomaya
gii-piboong.*

iskwaa	after
biboong	winter
ani	coming up in time, on the way
idash	and, but
aabawaa	warm weather, mild weather
wenji	for a certain reason, because
mikwendam	recollect, remember
dakaasin	be cooled by the wind

Making syrup is a lot of work. Sometimes it is hard
work but most of the time is spent just staring at the
fire, watching the sap so it doesn't burn. We spend
hours cutting firewood.

*Niibowa anokiiwin ayaamagad iskigamizigeng,
ozhichigaadeg zhiiwaagamizigan. Ayaanigodinong
zanagad i'iw anokiiwin, aanawi dash naaningodi-
nong ginwenzh ganawaabanjigaademagad eta i'iw
ishkode. Niibowa daso-diba'iganan nindazhiitaamin
maniseyaang.*

Niibowa	many, much
ozhichigaade	be made, be built
zhiiwaagamizigan	syrup
ayaangodinong	sometimes, occasionally
zanagad	be difficult, be hard (to manage)

aanawi	anyhow, although, despite, but
naanigodinong	now and then, sometimes, every once in a while
ginwenzh	for a long time
manise	cut firewood

I remember how my grampa used to keep the sap from boiling over. He hung a piece of salt pork over the hot sap. When it came up to boil over, it would get as far as the salt pork and go back down. It was easier than using a balsam branch.

Ingezikwenimaa nimishoomisiban gii-nagajitood ji ziigigamidesinig i'iw ziinzibaakwadaaboo. Ogii-agoodoon zhiiwitaagani gookoosh besho imaa enda ni iskigamideg i'iw ziinzibaakwadaaboo. Azhigwa apii wii-ziigigamideg, mii i'iw ziinzibaakwadaaboo dangiseg imaa zhiiwitaagani gookooshing mii ezhi-azheshkaag. Nawaj wenipanad ji ni aabajichigaadeg i'iw zhiiwitaagani gookoosh; nawaj dash zanagad naading iniw zhingobiin.

nimishoomis	my grandfather
ziigigamide	boil over
agoodoon	hang something
zhiiwitaagan	salt
gookoosh	pig, pork
ezhi	in a certain way, thus, so
azheshkaa	go backwards
naadin	go get something, fetch something
zhingobiin	balsam fir

I feel happy using my black kettle to boil sap. Just knowing that Indians all over northern Minnesota were making syrup like I was felt good.

Ninjiikendam aabajiitooyaan nimakade-akaadakikom ji ni iskigamizigeyaan. Mii onji i'iw gikendamaan miziwe Minisodakiing Anishinaabeg iskigamizigewaad, zhiiwaagamizigewaad; dibishkoo gayeniin ezichigeyaan mii wenji minwamanji'oyaan.

aabajiitoon	use something
nimakade-akaadaki-	
kom	my black kettle
miziwe	all over, everywhere
Minisodakiing	Minnesota
zhiiwaagamizige	make syrup
dibishkoo	just like, even , direct, equal

When we say we are of the earth, it is true. I think there is something in the maple syrup I need. It makes sense, countless generations of my ancestors depended on the syrup for food. I will continue to make syrup every spring.

Ikidoyang omaa akiing gidibendaagozimin; debweyendaagwad. Naanaagadawendamaan gegoo imaa ayaamagad imaa zhiiwaagamiziganing meneziyaan. Nisidawinaagoziwag ingiw ningetedanawemaaganag, mewinzha gaa-pimaadizijig, ogii-apenimodaanawaa i'iw zhiiwaagamizigan ji miijiwaad mii iw gaa onji-mino-ayaawaapan megwaa gii-pimaadiziwaad gaye wiinawaa. Apane ani ziigwang ninga-ozhiitoon ahiiwaagamizigan.

ikido	say, speak so
debweyendan	believe in something
gegoo	something, anything
ayaamagad	be (in a certain place), in a certain state
nisidawinaadiwag	they recognize each other
apenimo	depend on something, rely on something
megwaa	while, during
wiinawaa	they
apane	always, all the time, continually

We are thankful for the gift of syrup from the Creator.

Gimiigwechiwi'aanaan a'aw Gichi Manidoo atood zhiiwaagamizigan omaa akiing.

Gichi Manidoo	Great Spirit, God
omaa	here

I found a book that shows how some white guys do it. They have seven thousand taps connected with eight miles of plastic tubing. The sap is sucked from the trees using vacuum pumps. They expected to collect seventy thousand gallons of sap that would make seventeen hundred gallons of syrup. In the entire book, the phrase Native American is used just once.

It is always a family affair to go to the sugar bush. Anishinaabeg have been making syrup for hundreds of generations. We know who we were, who we are, and what to do each season. When the sun says it is sugar bush time, we gladly make syrup.

Ezigaa's first year actually started when he saw me making taps for the trees. Instead of looking at TV's Barney and Big Bird, my grandson's eyes followed the maple sticks that were drilled and carved into taps. He practiced counting them as he put the completed taps into a coffee can. The numbers he used didn't match the taps he was counting but that didn't matter because he was new at sugar bush and math. When Ezigaa went to the sugar bush for the first time, I saw the world anew again as I always do when I am watching two generations after me, my sons and grandsons, carry on our traditions.

We three left the house early. Patricia told Ezigaa that we were going to the deer's house and must be quiet when we are there.

When spending all day outside, it is easy to see winter turn into spring. At first, it is long-underwear cool in the mornings. The sun is bright on the hardly used snow. The snow is almost knee deep when we begin. It is crusty in the mornings, strong enough to support the weight of sap-gathering Shinnobs.

The cool wind wrapped around us as we showed Ezigaa how to find trees to tap. We found a good spot and started tapping. The trees were the right size and close together. There were no hills to climb. The sun had melted the snow at the bottom of the trees. The maples had a little brown collar of last fall's leaves, the emblems from the Canadian flag.

I was proud that Ezigaa knew to pause and leave an offering of tobacco at the base of each tree. From watching us, he knew how to thank the Creator for the gift of maple trees.

Using a hand drill, I drilled the holes at just the right height for a first-year tapper to get a good look. Ezigaa watched for a while, then handed me a twig to clean out the shavings. I put the tap in and the boy put a milk jug on the tap. After a few trees, he would tell me to hurry because he had a jug ready.

Standing back to survey our work, we watched the sap drip from the taps. Ezigaa looked at a couple of trees before he tried tasting it. He caught a few drops on his tongue and his smile was like warm sunshine to his gramma and grampa. As we trudged from tree to tree, Ezigaa danced along beside us on top of the snow. He was still looking for trees to tap as we followed the deer trail out of the woods.

The next morning we went back to see how much sap we had collected. On the way to the woods, I pointed out a bald eagle to Ezigaa. He didn't say a word, as if just seeing the brown and white bird was enough.

We were breaking through the crust of snow but Ezigaa was able to stay on top. He emptied the milk jugs into the buckets we carried. He was running from tree to tree.

Sometimes we boil the sap in the woods near the trees we tap. Other years we bring it home to boil. Our black cast iron kettle that takes us from ricing to sugar bush comes out again.

The fire we build invites participation. It begs to be poked and prodded so it burns better. Moving a piece of burning maple a quarter inch is sometimes necessary when tending a fire. Maybe it's just playing with fire, I don't know.

The steam coming off the sap suddenly appears for a few seconds, a sort of tentative start. Finally the steam is coming off steadily. It's like the sap finds the right amount of heat. The steam seems eager to be free. It billows out of the kettle, mingles with the wood smoke for a while, then disappears.

Brownish-colored foam begins to collect on top of the hot sap. It is skimmed off using an always handy balsam branch. The bubbling, boiling sap chuckles to itself once in a while as it cooks down.

As the sap boils down, more is added. The sap, almost syrup, roils in the kettle. The fire burns on all day until we have no more sap to add. We know that sitting around a fire is a good place to tell stories and hold your grandson on your lap.

Ezigaa tasted it as it got sweeter and sweeter. After about the 134th time, we decided we were done for the day. He stood back as we lifted the kettle from the fire. We took the syrup inside where we filtered it. The golden brown syrup was warm when we poured it over the pancakes. The best part of spring is teaching Ezigaa something he can pass on to his own grandchildren when the time comes. For now, Ezigaa takes sugar bush taps to school for Show and Tell.

As spring gives way to summer, we start planning to hit the powwow trail. Patricia sometimes has a food stand where she makes her award-winning frybread. When she doesn't want to cook, she dances. Both of us enjoy the socializing that goes on at modern-day powwows. We visit, lie about our children and grandchildren.

"Yup, my son is a hunter. He went hunting the other day and shot a deer. The bullet passed through and hit a mallard on the other side. The duck fell in the lake and scared a walleye which jumped into the canoe. Yup, that boy is a hunter."

It's tough planning a summer, so we don't do it. There are always too many choices to make. Should we go to that Leech Lake powwow or the one in Wisconsin?

One summer we ruled out the close places because it wasn't enough of a challenge for our Rez car. That was the year we were driving the old '67 Buick. The same old grandfather Buick my cousin, Chuck Greensky, calls Five Deer. He gave it that name after looking at the size of the trunk. The trunk was easy to open, I just used the dipstick or a screwdriver. One part of the car I liked was the capacity—we slept four little kids on the seats. It was a big blue metal tent that protected them from the storms that sometimes follow us on the powwow trail. That old car always looked right when it was full. When the Shinnobs start piling out, it looks like a clown car.

Summer powwows come in all sizes, vary in distance from home, and bring together a different set of Shinnobs each time, but a few elements are the same. A drum and singers and dancers in a circle are the basic ingredients.

I remembered asking my grampa if he was going to a powwow at one of the local colleges. He asked how many drums would be there. I told him sixteen or seventeen different drums were coming. He thought about it awhile and then told me they only needed one. I laughed and thought that shows how dances have changed over the years.

The drum will synchronize everyone's heartbeat. There are always more smiles than frowns at a powwow. Everyone is welcome at a powwow, you don't have to be an Indian to enjoy what is going on.

Most powwows have several drums, head dancers, and American flags. There are booths of traders selling their wares, food stands offering wild rice and frybread in addition to the traditional hamburgers, mini-donuts, and snowcones. The doings are guided somewhat by a powwow committee and a Master of Ceremonies.

My sister, Nita Northrup Fineday, developed a checklist for the things we see and hear at a powwow.

Eagle flying over	✓
Bone whistle lecture	✓
Lost kids found	✓
Dropped eagle feather	✓
Honor songs	✓
Tape recorders around the drums	✓
Old friends	✓
New friends	✓
Relatives	✓
Ex-wives or -husbands	✓
New relatives	✓
Blanket raffle	✓
Giveaways	✓
Long winded M.C.	✓

Every powwow has its moments. The M.C. might explain that they are having a little problem in the development of Frybread Lite due to the use of USDA surplus commodity flour in the mix. Because of the high protein count of the worms, they will have to start from scratch again. The giveaways for the dancers and community members include everything from a piece of Tupperware to a quart of oil for those driving Rez cars.

One of the things I have noticed about powwows is a new tradition that I am not sure fits in with the old ways. Princess contests are now popular. Some pow-wows have five or more young women wearing a sash and a crown. The sash identifies them as the current Princess representing their school, Reservation, pow-wow, or tribe.

On one hand, I think our young women should be recognized for their accomplishments but maybe, just maybe, we are doing it the wrong way.

First, why a Princess? Isn't that a concept borrowed from the Europeans, the royalty ranking system that came from their world? I think one of the major reasons the Europeans came to this continent was to escape the rigid class structure of their homeland, where birth counted for more than individual merit.

Are we so hard up for traditions that we have to use one of these discarded ideas? Who started the Princess contests anyway? It looks like a dead-end job being a Princess. I never hear of anyone going on to become a Queen.

But, for many of the young women, we have had Princess contests as long as they can remember. It is traditional in their lives.

There must be a better way to honor our young women, the life givers of the next generation.

I've been to many powwows over the years. Some were for ceremonial reasons, some for political reasons, but most were just for social reasons. Like the seasons themselves, they bring back the stories we use to teach and remember our history.

One of the most powerful political powwows in recent memory was one held in International Falls, Minnesota. The Anishinaabeg were gathering to commemorate the Jay Treaty, the agreement that calls for freedom of movement of indigenous people across the border between the United States and Canada.

In the old days, this would have made the settlers nervous because there were two thousand Shinnobs gathering, half from the U.S. and half from Canada. Drums and singers from both countries were there. It is proof that the power of singing carries across the years and imaginary lines.

Anishinaabeg from both sides of the imaginary line made sandwiches, arranged for media coverage, lined up transportation, and prepared the spiritual and traditional gifts to exchange. Gift bundles of wild rice, smoked fish, sweet grass, and sage moved from hand to hand at the gathering.

Rallying to support our right to cross the border is more important than many people might think. My family and I had some personal experiences with U.S. Customs on a trip to Winnipeg and back. We were waved through on our way across the border going into Canada. On the way back is when we met U.S. Customs.

Maybe we were stopped because our car was wearing Fond du Lac Reservation license plates or maybe it was a slow day.

The man with the gun told us to pull our car off to the side and come inside. When I walked in, the first thing I saw was a large picture of the American president. It reminded me that this was the same outfit that blew the hell out of Iraq in the Gulf War.

Guys with guns were milling around the office. One of them told us to surrender the keys to the car. My wife, my son Joseph, and I were taken to separate rooms. We knew we hadn't broken any laws but just being around all those guys with guns was scary. What if one of them was having a bad day?

We gave up our identification papers when they demanded them. The first gun searching us was joined by a second gun who blocked the door of the small room. We emptied our pockets and removed our moccasins at their command. In the other room, my wife was dumping her purse on the table. She later told us one gun grabbed a McDonalds's coffee stirrer that fell out of her purse. He examined the small plastic straw closely, maybe looking for drugs or weapons. The guys with the guns were very thorough in their search.

It felt like a scene from a bad Gestapo movie. It didn't feel like the United States I knew. It was like we had to prove that we weren't crooks or smugglers. I thought a body cavity search was next but they didn't go that far. When they couldn't find any reason to hold us, they let us go.

We drove in silence for fifty miles or so. Once we got far enough down the road, we began talking about our experience. We should have had such a system in place when the white guys first got here. Christopher Columbus would have had to declare that he was not carrying drugs, weapons, or weird diseases. Everyone else who came after him would have had to declare the same thing. It sure would have been a different country if we had invented a customs office.

How does the Declaration of Independence describe us?

> ". . . the merciless Indian savages whose known rule of warfare is an undistinguished destruction of all ages, sexes, and conditions."

Powwows keep the culture alive. They are a time for us to celebrate and remember the people and places important to the Anishinaabeg. Like our language, the dances and giveaways were once banned by the United States. We hold on to our traditions and give gifts to honor our guests, our elders, and our leaders. Some powwows include giveaways that mark the end of a year of mourning. We are reminded it is important to be generous.

What is Indian Summer?

It's that warm spell between Indian Spring and Indian Fall.

Traveling takes us right into fall and winter sometimes. It can become an occupation in its own right. I've had some interesting experiences and each place has taught me something about the world and the people I share it with.

On an educational adventure, we motored to Washington, D.C. The Bureau of Indian Affairs called and wanted to hear some quips and comments from my newspaper column as part of American Indian Heritage Month.

Who invented the Bureau of Indian Affairs?

Someone who was really mad at us.

I was kind of worried at first. Uh oh, summoned to Washington by the Bureau of Indian Affairs. I didn't

have any Affairs to be ashamed of, so I went. It was a little before Veterans Day so the places we wanted to see
weren't crowded. We first went to the Wall to honor
those who died in the Vietnam War.

We took care of the necessary business with the BIA
and then became tourists. We walked to the Washington
Monument where we eyeballed the district. The elevator
operator stopped the car and showed us a piece of pipestone that was mounted inside the monument. He told
us the pipestone was from Minnesota and asked what
tribe we were from. My wife said Dakota, my son Joseph
said Chippewa, my sister Doris said Ojibwe, and I said
I was a Shinnob.

We walked to the Smithsonian then walked all over
inside the buildings. We walked to the Lincoln Memorial. We walked back to the Air and Space Museum. We
walked around Arlington Cemetery and the Marine
Corps Iwo Jima statue. We did so much walking my son
renamed the place. For him, it will forever be known as
Walkington, D.C.

We drove across the Potomac River to see Princess
Pale Moon. She is a woman who got in trouble because
she couldn't prove her claims of being an Indian. With
this in mind, we went to visit her at the American Heritage Foundation, which she founded in 1973.

The foundation claims to be the largest privately supported nonprofit American Indian organization in the
country. In her brochures, Princess Pale Moon claims to
be Cherokee and Ojibwe.

One of the things the foundation is proud of is their
sponsorship of the Miss Indian U.S.A. pageant every
year. Princess Pale Moon is the president of the foundation and her husband, Dr. Wil Rose, is the chief execu-

tive officer. Her two sons also work for the foundation. Dr. Rose gave us some background information about Princess Pale Moon and the foundation's efforts. We learned that the Princess dresses in some kind of tribal regalia to sing the national anthem for the Washington Redskins football team. I don't know what to call such a person—is her first name Princess or Pale?

After talking with Dr. Rose and hearing the grand plans for the foundation, we met Princess Pale. She was well dressed in white people's clothes and was wearing a lot of turquoise. She was charming and smiled a lot while we were talking. It looked like she was wearing some kind of dark makeup on her skin.

If you're an Indian, why is your skin so light?

Melanin Deficit Disorder.

She gave me a book about her life but I couldn't find a connection to the Ojibwe. Further, there was no explanation on how she became a princess.

We left the foundation and Walkington, D.C., knowing more about how we can be ripped off. It's hard to dislike people like the Princess and her family, but what they are doing is wrong—pretending to be Indian when they are not. We don't need her foundation or pageant to boost our pride. Singing the national anthem for a racist mascot organization is questionable also. Before we left, Princess, or Pale, bought some wild rice from us. We charged her the standard white guy price. I guess after she reads this she won't be buying any more rice from us. Too bad. If she really is a princess, she can command one of her subjects to grow some. In my opin-

ion, Princess Pale Moon is as real an Indian as paddy
rice is wild.

My family can't always travel with me and my car
doesn't always start, but that doesn't stop me from getting around. One winter I rode the dog to the Twin
Cities. It'd been years since I'd ridden the Greyhound
bus.

It was the usual winter dead car story. Mine was in the
shop and the relatives who could have given me a ride
were working or their cars weren't. It was too far to walk
and the trains don't run anymore.

How did you know he was a regular hitch-
hiker?

He used a suitcase made from a five-gallon gas
can.

My sister, Nita, dropped me off at the ticket agent's
office in Cloquet, Minnesota. I waved good-bye to her
and went in and paid for my $18 ticket. I browsed the
magazine rack while waiting for the 12:40 P.M. bus.

The gray, silver, black, and blue bus pulled in on
time. The driver, wearing his snazzy gray uniform, got
out and told the waiting people the bus was full. He said
it was standing room only until Hinckley, Minnesota, an
hour away, when two seats would become available. The
only other alternative was to wait six hours for the next
bus. I couldn't wait, I had to get to the Cities.

I got on the bus first because in addition to needing a
ride, I needed to use the bathroom. I really had to go.

I used the toilet and joined the others standing in the aisle. The standing passengers were holding on to the seats and luggage rack as the bus swayed around the corners. I held on, thinking—stand all the way to the Cities? The whole idea seemed silly. I had paid as much for my ticket as the people sitting in the soft seats.

I knew where there was an empty seat—the restroom. I closed the lid on the blue water tank and sat down. It didn't smell too bad in there. The seat was hard plastic but it was better than standing and swaying for hours.

I propped the door open with my briefcase to let the other passengers know I was a social animal. The nearest ones smiled when they saw how I had solved my problem of standing all the way.

I looked around my private sitting room. It was a mostly steel and glass cubical. The main window was frosted and all I could see was light and shadows. I propped the smaller window open so I could get fresh air. I couldn't see much except snowbanks but did feel like I could control my environment.

I used a Greyhound moist towellette to wedge the light on because it goes out when the door is open.

The vibrations from the bus motor and transmission travel just fine through the plastic seat. I was almost beginning to enjoy the buzz. My butt got numb after about sixty miles so I stood for a while.

After reading the signs posted in the bathroom, I opened my briefcase and took out a newspaper. I opened it full width and read. That was when I realized I had more room than the other forty-seven passengers. Four people still stood in the aisle, looking like silent tour guides.

Greyhound bus #5056 roared on down Interstate 35.

The vibrations from the seat were still pleasant. I stood again because I was enjoying the buzz too much. I thought of those vibrating motel beds that cost a quarter. When I was finished with my newspaper, I was a little sleepy so I took a power nap draped over the sink. I didn't even have to worry about drooling.

After the smoke break at the Grand Casino in Hinckley, the other passengers began using my bathroom. My private sitting room wasn't so private anymore. While waiting for them to get done, I saw perfect strangers' butts rubbing up and down the aisle. I was careful to air the place out after each visitor. In spite of the benefits of the private sitting room, I was glad when the driver came on the PA and announced the next stop was St. Paul.

Overall the ride wasn't too bad. The vibrating seat ends up in the same place as the cushioned ones. The ride was more Spartan but we all got there at the same time. It could have been worse. What if I'd had to stand on top of the bus all the way to the Cities?

I got off that bus, walked away, and never looked back.

Occasionally we'll fly somewhere. When I went to New York City for a clean water conference, I learned my suspenders set off the metal detector at the airport. I took them off and held up my pants while I walked through. I found my seat and hoped we wouldn't be like those airplanes in the headlines that apparently try to fly underground.

When I arrived in New York, the Big Apple, I saw how big it really was. There were thousands of people I didn't know. I got a room at the Washington Square Hotel and learned that Bob Dylan and Joan Baez used to live there. After unpacking, I went out to get a close look at the city.

I walked across the street to Washington Square Park to hang out and have a look around. While sitting on one of the benches, I noticed the police surrounding and sealing off the park. I wasn't worried. I knew I had paid that parking ticket from 1976, the last time I was in the city.

It turns out they weren't looking for me. They were after drug dealers who had been under surveillance all day. A man tried to run and was thrown to the ground right in front of me. The undercover cop took out his gun and pressed it to the man's head. He said, "Don't move, don't move."

This was happening just a few feet in front of me. It was about the same distance I sit from my TV at home. This wasn't TV, this was real. The man on the ground said in a shaky voice, "I'm not moving, I'm not moving."

I stood up and in a quivering voice said, "I am, I am," while moving out of the line of fire. I turned and walked away thinking, been in New York for five whole hours before I saw my first gun. It was a lot different than life back on my quiet Reservation. I had to put my city eyes on real quick to adapt.

New York is busy, almost like everyone had two cups of coffee before they hit the ground, running. They talk fast too: 100 words a minute with gusts up to 150. While I was there, I ate at a nice restaurant on Fifth Avenue. Being a Shinnob, I ordered the rabbit dish. Fifteen bucks for a little bitty bowl of something that could be rabbit. There were just a couple of pieces floating around in the bowl, about as much meat as on one hindquarter. I wanted to leave a snare as a tip but didn't have one with me.

The highlight of the trip was a visit with Bob Holman, poet. I met him while working on a project called, "The United States of Poetry."

Is that really a poem or
did you just make it up?

Yes.

Bob Holman showed me his digs at the Nuyorican Poet's Cafe. I stood up on my hind legs and recited poetry to the East Village crowd. The people listened and laughed like they do back home.

I ran into Anishinaabe poet Diane Burns at the Poet's Cafe. It felt like home to hear her say, *"Boozhoo."* (Hello.)

I gave her some of our wild rice because I didn't know what kind of a ricing season they'd had in New York.

Not all my trips are full of friendly people. Some strangers rush past curious and head straight for racist when they see a Shinnob. One time, my wife Patricia and I motored to Bemidji State University in Minnesota. We found out how little people know about others in their midst.

We were in town to get details about a racist professor. We wanted to support our friends who had made a formal complaint. There is no need to repeat what the professor was saying, it is enough to know he would have been punched out at any Indian bar in the state. He would have been laughed off the grounds at any Indian gathering.

Upon arriving at the university, we decided to lunch at the student union. It was close to noon so most of the tables were full. There were eating students, studying students, and talking students spread out all over the big room. We saw an almost-empty table occupied by one man. The brown table had seven empty chairs. As my wife approached the table, the man, white and older than us, snarled, "You can't sit there."

She asked if the table was reserved. He didn't answer, he just kept repeating, "You can't sit there."

His voice was getting louder and more angry sounding. The students sitting around him began to look at the scene. The Shinnob students at the next table were watching the event real closely.

He didn't see me standing behind him. I went through my list of options. I thought of slapping him for the way he was talking to my wife. Nope, didn't want to go to jail over it. I just settled for growling at him. I asked him to use a civil tone. He ignored me so I leaned closer to his hearing aid and growled again. This time he heard me, maybe because I was growling through clenched teeth.

He quit talking mean to my wife but still wouldn't let us sit at the empty table. After we figured out he wasn't joking, we wondered who he was? He seemed like a very angry man.

We didn't return his anger, just crowded in with the Shinnob students. The food tasted better with them around anyway. The angry white man was identified as a janitor who worked there. We were glad to learn he wasn't the official greeter for the university.

After eating with the students, we left. But before leaving, we laughed in Ojibwe and Dakota at the man.

We saw him an hour later, still sitting alone, and all the racist remarks began to make sense. Both the professor and the janitor had an attitude that fit a pattern. Cultural diversity is okay, as long as the Indians sit at another table.

Most of my travels aren't tainted by racism but its ugly face is always lurking nearby. We have a lot of work ahead of us confronting racism and educating those who think or wish we had died in the last century.

The boundaries imposed on us need to be ignored. Like the powwow held to unite the Anishinaabeg of the U.S. and Canada, we need to reach out to tribes everywhere on this continent. We have more in common with our indigenous relatives in Mexico City than we do with Princess Pale Moon in Washington, D.C.

We journeyed to Mexico City to take part in a rally for indigenous people's rights. Capturing the entire experience is difficult but a few images will always linger.

Mexico City is large. We flew over a lot of city before we got to the airport. It is a valley, 7500 feet above sea level in the mountains. There is a severe air pollution problem. The thin and dirty air was a shock to my rural Minnesota lungs.

It is mostly a stone city, prone to periodic earthquakes, floods, and droughts. It has an ancient and violent past. Mexico has a lot of history and we saw some of it at the Pyramid of the Sun.

The Mexico City traffic is thick, rush hour all day. Big, smoking Dina diesel buses mingle with the orange and white Volkswagen taxis. Trucks of all sizes keep the pedestrians running. We learned quickly that pedestrians do not have the right-of-way in that traffic.

Try to picture six lanes of traffic using a three-lane street. Dashing across the streets became our daily exercise. Speed bumps are scattered liberally throughout the city. We discovered that speed bumps are a good place to cross the street.

Hola means *boozhoo, gracias* means *miigwech*. We didn't know Spanish before we left but we quickly learned how to say, "Where is the bathroom?"

It felt strangely pleasant to be dark-haired, dark-skinned, where the majority of the people were dark-haired, dark-skinned.

Mexico is a land of contrasts. The rich live near the poor. There are walls within walls, stone courtyards with tropical looking plants.

On a busy street corner, we saw a young, fashionably dressed woman talking on a cellular phone. Squatting right behind her was an old woman with milky eyes, holding her hand out to the passing people. As we walked the city streets, we saw someone selling trinkets every couple of feet. Our new diet of refried beans made us jet-propelled pedestrians.

Fortunately, we didn't have to spend all of our time in the city. We used public transportation to get out in the countryside. We knew we were leaving because we began seeing blue sky again. Vendors would get on the bus at every little village to sell peanuts, Coke, bread, and toys.

Once out in the countryside, we began seeing burros, cows, and horses walking anywhere they wanted. That would explain the massive grills on the trucks we were seeing. The two-lane road had potholes that served the same purpose as the speed bumps in the city.

We came through a village that was the same size as

ours back on the Fond du Lac Reservation. There were quite a few satellite dishes on the red clay roofs. A woman walked past us; she had a propane tank in a shawl on her back. A shawl around her front held a young baby. We saw women hanging out clothes to dry on cacti.

Our destination was a hacienda called Tepetitlan. For 275 years, the hacienda has stood witness to history as have the surrounding Mazahua people. Part of the hacienda was destroyed in the revolution of the 1920s. Now the hacienda is the home of Amextra, an organization that helps empower the Mazahua people. Students come to be trained as the leaders of the next century; some have gone on to study at the major universities. There is hope and planning for the future going on at the hacienda. We were glad to witness a small part of it.

We left the hacienda to meet people in their homes. Everyone shakes hands, from the youngest to the oldest. It is not a bone-crushing grip, just a gentle touching of the flesh, just like the old people back home. We felt lucky to shake so many hands of the hands that surround the city, hands that hold the history of the land.

From our cousins in Canada to our distant relatives in Mexico, we learn the gentle power of continued presence. We move through the seasons like our ancestors moved through the woods and across the waters put here by the Creator. We use modern methods to keep the old traditions alive.

The pleasures of being a grampa still surprise me as I explain my history, the history of the Anishinaabeg, to the next generation of storytellers, ricers, basket makers,

hunters, and travelers. By gathering the stories throughout the year, I can mark the places we have been and expand the limits of where we can go. We may not be
home in the city, but Anishinaabeg faces will turn up in
the most surprising places.

3
Racism

ODE EWINENIMOWINISH WAA

As an Anishinaabe in northern Minnesota, I feel acts of racism almost every day. It comes in many shades and variations. The following examples are not the worst ones, they are just a reminder that I cannot escape the ugliness.

Some years back, I was bringing my son, Joseph, home from the babysitter. He was belted in his car seat and I stopped for a traffic light in downtown Duluth. While waiting, I was playing with him because I hadn't seen him all day. I was trying to make him laugh, he was smiling back at me when I felt someone's eyes on me. I looked up and saw a white woman in the next traffic lane staring at us.

I looked back at her and she quickly looked away. She then surreptitiously locked her car door. She had to reach under her left arm with her right hand to reach the door lock. I saw one finger come out and push down on the lock. I told my son to lock his door.

I wondered who had more reason to be afraid?

Once I wanted to buy a jacket. I had studied the ads and knew exactly what kind of jacket I wanted. It was made of Gore-Tex and would be used for three seasons of the year. I went to a department store just off the Rez in Cloquet. There I found the jacket I wanted in my price range. I was trying to decide on the color when I felt someone grab my arm. The white store clerk had my sleeve pinched between her fingers and was trying to lead me off. While pulling, she told me the cheaper jackets were at the other end of the rack.

I pulled free and told the clerk I could afford the jacket I was looking at. I then asked her to guess if I would buy a jacket from her? She didn't want to guess. I went to another store where the clerk didn't judge my wallet by my skin color. I got the jacket and respect I was looking for.

One evening I took my family out to eat. We were celebrating payday, a sometimes scarce event. While waiting for the hostess to seat us, I noticed that everyone had stopped eating to stare at us. Everyone—old people, young people, babies in high chairs—were looking at us. I didn't see one friendly face. They were looking at us like we owed them a great deal of money.

I did a quick check. All members of my family were wearing clothes. I decided they were staring because we were Shinnobs. It felt cold, like standing in a meat market cooler.

I pointed my index finger on top of my head and swiveled around. I wanted to give them a 360 degree view of this Shinnob. I noticed my son was doing the same thing as me. Our actions must have embarrassed them because they started eating again. During the meal, we could feel eyes on us as we ate. The meal was one stare-down contest after another. We won each time because we have had more experience in dealing with racism.

In my travels, I came across a leaflet that was being passed out in the Bemidji, Minnesota, area. The leaflet details the rules for hunting Minnesota Indians. The new season came about because of the scarcity of big game. The leaflet calls for a limit of two Indians, either sex, per white hunter. It contains suggestions for finding Indians near liquor stores, welfare offices, and mailboxes on the first of the month. The season is open all year long. The leaflet is similar to the ones passed out in Wisconsin during the spearfishing wars. Those annual wars came about when a federal judge said treaty rights do exist. The white bigots came to the boat landings to harass and intimidate Indians who were using their treaty rights to spearfish in the springtime. There was random gunfire and pipe bombs were found at some landings. Bigots were using slingshots to shoot steel ball bearings at the Indians who were spearing. The Indians were not intimidated and kept spearing.

I have been to the boat landings and seen the fury of racism there. "Save a walleye, spear a Indian," [sic] or "Save two walleye, spear a pregnant squaw." Signs like these let me know precisely how these people feel. It is hard to talk to someone who is chanting over and over, "Timber Nigger, Timber Nigger."

But it is almost refreshing to see people acting like they really feel. Blatant racism is always easier to face than closet bigotry.

Closet bigots are everywhere. They can be found in business, in government, and in education. I shudder when I read in the local newspaper that, "The North Dakota Fighting Sioux Beat the UMD Bulldogs."

College sports teams using tribal people as mascots send a message to our children that we are less than human.

The closet bigots can be found in the media, too. I wince when our tribal names are mispronounced by the local TV news crews. I change stations when I hear racist jokes on the radio. Ask any Shinnob and they can tell similar stories about racism in Minnesota. Just be careful when asking because it is a subject laced with anger and passion on both sides.

One person who took both sides was Bud Grant, former coach of the Minnesota Vikings football team. Coach Grant mounted the steps of the state capital to protest against the treaty rights of the Anishinaabeg. He showed one of his true colors. The Coach doesn't bother us, we have confronted two-faced people before. We know from the old stories that the treaties will always be under attack. Coach is the latest in a long line of treaty haters. He favors abrogating treaties.

Want to get rid of the treaties? So do I. We'll go back to the way things were before the treaties were signed. We'd have to ask everyone to leave Minnesota unless they were Dakota or Anishinaabeg. That would include the Minnesota Vikings, of course. Coach Grant could lead the charge out of here.

But before they left, I would ask one small favor. Clean up the mess you made. Put it back to the way it was when you first came here.

Coach Grant moans about the potential loss of walleye fishing in Mille Lacs Lake if the Anishinaabeg win the treaty rights fight. I have seen the bottom of that lake while spearfishing. The trash that has accumulated should make us all ashamed. Instead of fighting about treaty rights, let's band together and clean up the lakes. I'd help, I have a canoe and another spear.

Ironically, I found a book with a picture of Coach Grant on the cover. I was strolling through a mall in Bemidji, Minnesota, when I stopped in a bookstore. The book was on top of a pile of others on the discount table. The book was called *Homeless Dreams*, and it showed Coach Grant wearing a beaded hat with feathers. The kind of a hat they call a war bonnet in the movies. I thought the face paint Coach was wearing was a bit much. In the book, Coach says, "Now that I am retired from coaching, I have the opportunity to spend more time doing what I like to do outdoors, such as hunting, fishing, and camping, etc.

"As a boy growing up, I would have liked to live with the Indians and experienced their way of life. It always bothered me that in the movies they were always the bad guys and always lost the fights they were in. I wanted to help them win. I feel that way about the homeless."

Now Coach, as they used to say in the old Perry Mason movies, "Exactly when were you lying?"

Was it when you were on the capital steps protesting against Indians or was it in the book when you wanted the Indians to win?

Coach, do you still want to experience life with the Indians? I could arrange a visit here on the Fond du Lac Reservation. I would show you what our life is really like, maybe tell you a few stories about when we did win the fights.

It's too bad Coach didn't accept my invitation to come to the Rez. If he had, we wouldn't be hearing the garbage he is putting out now.

Someone gave me a copy of Coach's latest effort, the Bud Grant Report. I learned that he is now going to be submitting guest columns to newspapers.

It is a "continuing effort to have balanced reporting on the treaty rights issue here in Minnesota."

In his announcement to the editors, Coach says, "I, and those who question treaty claims, have been wrongfully portrayed as racist, ignorant and anti-Indian."

Coach Grant promises to submit columns that are, "thought provoking, newsworthy, and factually based perspectives on tribal claims to treaty rights and sovereignty."

C'mon Coach, the Super Bowl is over. The judge in this federal district says we have hunting, fishing, and gathering rights in the ceded territories. The ceded territories are in Minnesota, Wisconsin, and Michigan. The 1837 and 1854 Treaties are valid because the Anishinaabeg specifically reserved those rights when they signed the documents.

As a Fonjalacker (Rez slang) I must respond to the Bud Grant Report, Update #1. I will call it the Fond du Lac Update on the Bud Grant Update. We could shorten it to FDLUOTBGU. The initials don't make sense and neither does Coach.

My offer to get together and clean up the lakes in Minnesota is still on the table.

Coach's column starts off with a bold headline that says, "Tribal Claims to Sovereignty and Special Rights Off-Reservation Are Being Defeated Nationwide."

He ends the column by begging for money. Coach says his organization called PERM has raised $320,000 for legal costs and needs another $1,500,000 to pay witnesses, lawyers, and for research. That seems a bit steep to me. I wonder what Coach's anti-treaty group members are getting for their money? PERM is a nonprofit organization. Does this mean their books are open to the public? Who are the PERM lawyers?

The column is filled with half truths, half lies, and other distortions. I can hardly wait to see the silliness called the Bud Grant Report, Update #2.

I still wish Coach would have taken me up on my invitation to visit. Since he didn't, I will not ask him to visit; instead, I will debate with him. So here's the challenge: I will debate Coach Bud Grant anywhere, anytime about treaty rights. I guarantee we will have a Super Bowl of a time.

Sports seems to breed racism.

The 1995 World Series between the Atlanta Braves and the Cleveland Indians is another glaring example. I like baseball but the screwball idea of using us as mascots is an error. In my field of dreams, it wouldn't happen.

I balk at the idea of seeing the tomahawk chop on TV again. I strike out when trying to explain what it means to my grandson. I walk when I see fans wearing turkey feathers and paint on their faces. I am forced out of the room when I see fans waving foam tomahawks.

Those who think we are being honored by using racist mascot symbols must have a franchise on stupidity. They have sacrificed their common sense and will never enter my Hall of Fame. Personally, I think those responsible for demeaning mascots should be wrapped in wet horsehide and confined in a batting cage.

My family and I were at the World Series game when the Braves were playing the Minnesota Twins for the championship in 1991. We were pitching an educational message but no one was catching. Nevertheless, I will continue to fight against racism even if we have to go into extra innings. I hope we can continue to advance on this important issue. I want to get rid of the spikes of racism. America needs a change-up in its attitude toward the original people of this continent.

There are hundreds of tribes of indigenous people. In spite of our differences, we must form a league to combat this evil. We must shut out racism every time we see or feel it. We are not rookies, we are veterans because we have hundreds of years of experiences.

I bet Pete Rose would like the idea of respecting each other even more than we do now. I think Joe Jackson would have given up his shoes if it would help. Even Jackie Robinson would break into major leagues of happiness if we struck out racism in baseball. I would give Kirby Puckett a pennant to wave if we got rid of racist mascots. If Ted Turner had a single idea to change the double-faced attitudes toward us, I would have triple the respect I have for him now. We could run home and tell our children. Joe DiMaggio had a smile on his face after hitting in fifty-six consecutive games, mine would be even bigger if we didn't have to hear the Hey-ya song anymore. I don't even want to talk about Chiefs Noc a Homa and Wahoo.

One reason given for not changing the team names is the cost of such an undertaking. In these days of multi-million-dollar players and stadiums, that doesn't make sense. I know someone would make money if the uniforms and nicknames changed. Who says it is good business to demean us? How many times do we have to tell the owners we don't like what they do to us in the name of sports?

Some people say this is a small issue and we should spend our time and energy on more important things. But I say we must strike out against racism regardless of what form it takes.

The World Series is the end of the baseball season for the year but football is on deck. Next, we have to wind up against the Redskins, among others. I am proud to let my children and grandchildren know that I took a stance against racism. I want them to know that racism is not the great American pastime. When I go on road trips, I am reminded that racists are always around.

I was working at a small theater in Albert Lea, Minnesota, where I was acting in a one-man show I'd written. I stepped outside of the theater to have a smoke during a rehearsal break. A carload of white people went by. When they saw me, they gave out a long series of war whoops. I showed them the back of my hand and gave them one half of the peace sign. It ended there but I had to be prepared to fight if they decided to come back and escalate matters.

I find it hard to explain racism to my young ones. We make a game of spotting racists. The people who cross the street so they don't have to meet us are worth a laugh. The store clerk who won't touch us when handing back change is a daily reminder that racism is both old and new. I hope I can teach my young ones how to cope and overcome racism. My grandson, Ezigaa, at six years old is already aware of racism. He sometimes points it out to me when he feels it.

What is a hard-luck Chimmook? (Rez slang for white man)

A bigot compulsive gambler who lives on a lake
that has spearing and a casino.

In spite of the racism I have felt from white people, I
do not believe all white people are bigots, closet or oth-
erwise. I know too many fine people who are not like
that. It is my hope that we can use education and understanding to change racial attitudes. We have a long
way to go but it has only been five hundred years since
we met the white man. We have made some progress. At
least, the United States government is no longer en-
couraging citizens to shoot us.

At the Black Bear, one of the casinos owned and man-
aged by the Fond du Lac Band of Lake Superior
Chippewa, I overheard a white employee asking, *"Now*
what do them Indians want?"

It was such a good question, I thought I would try and
answer whether the employee was ready to listen or not.

We want respect. If that employee can't or doesn't
understand us, maybe he shouldn't be working there.
There are Shinnobs in the casino everyday. Some might
even be the employee's boss. It has got to be hard looking down on someone while kissing up.

Actually, we want the same things everyone else
wants. We are humans and share the same basic needs
such as air, water, food, shelter, and security for our
children.

Another thing we want is recognition of our rights.
The usual human rights and those guaranteed in the
United States Constitution and treaties. As original in-
habitants of this continent, we have dual citizenship.
We are citizens of our tribal groups and also citizens of
the United States. Each kind of citizenship carries cer-

tain rights and responsibilities. They are mostly the same but different with respect to treaty rights. A lot of people think the rights in the treaties were granted by the United States. They are wrong. We reserved the rights when the documents were signed. We are not a conquered people. When the treaties were signed, we were the military power in the region. I frequently hear treaties called nineteenth-century documents, implying they are no longer valid in the twentieth or twenty-first centuries. I remind them the U.S. Bill of Rights is an eighteenth-century document that is still valid. The treaties are the law of the land. If that employee or any-one else wants to know what we want, it's simple. Read the treaties, we do. But then again, I can hear Mitch Walking Elk, a songwriter who sings, "and when they want what we got, they just change the laws."

A man who ran afoul of the one of the laws was John Gauthier-Taborshak. He is one of my friend, Betty Jack's, extended family. She is an Anishinaabe woman who is enrolled at Lac Court Oreilles Reservation in Wisconsin. Each Reservation determines their own membership requirements and they create a list of members who qualify for inclusion on the tribal rolls.

John was driving to work at the Hole in the Wall casino when he was trailed by Wisconsin Department of Natural Resources game wardens. They stopped him in the casino parking lot. After talking awhile, the game wardens took away John's eagle feather.

We look on eagle feathers as a connection between the indigenous people and the Creator. The feathers are used in various ceremonies and some say the eagle is a messenger from the Creator.

The Wisconsin game wardens gave him a receipt and told him he would be hearing from the federal government.

Now they are holding the eagle feather hostage until the enrolled Winnebago (the Winnebago now call themselves Ho Chunk) can prove he is enrolled. Warden David Zeug told the newspapers there is extra sensitivity about eagles these days because of eighteen eagles that were found poisoned in northern Wisconsin. Zeug admitted that the poisoned eagles had all of their feathers. No arrests have been made in the poisoning of the eagles and no suspects have been identified.

Mike Chosa, everyone's uncle, told John they would still be rolling around in the parking lot if they tried to take his eagle feather.

So what is this? Is it a stupid mistake by the game wardens or the beginning of a new religious war? According to a story in the Duluth newspaper, "Warden Zeug said his department fully recognizes the rights of Indians to possess eagle feathers. But it is in everyone's best interest that the possession be monitored, to protect the eagles and tribal members' access to them."

David Duncan, he of Feathergate fame, as the even more notorious Nahganub/Bresette case came to be called, said the federal policy is that, "Indians can possess eagle feathers."

Further, Duncan stated, "There would be no attempt to prosecute and he (John Gauthier-Taborshak) wouldn't lose his feathers."

Duncan is the enforcement officer for the U.S. Fish and Wildlife Service stationed in Duluth. The Feathergate case involved two Shinnobs. Esther Nahganub makes and sells dreamcatchers and she sometimes uses feathers in her creations. Walt Bressette had a retail shop in the Duluth Miller Hill Mall. He was selling Esther's work. While on routine patrol in the mall, Duncan observed what he called violations of the Migratory Bird Act. Esther Nahganub's creations were confiscated by Duncan, but after a federal trial he had to return them because the judge said Indians have individual treaty rights to possess feathers.

It is frightening to know that this could happen to any Shinnob who drives through Wisconsin. Who declared that state an eagle-feather-free zone? The boat landing protests are behind us now so this must be the new battleground in the ongoing war.

They got the land, the trees, and water. Now, they want our spirituality. Maybe the game wardens were seeking the spirituality found in eagle feathers.

I know what we could do to help the game wardens. Invite them to a powwow. There they could find more eagle feathers than they could shake a nightstick at. The game wardens could stand near the entrance where the dancers come in during grand entry. The game wardens could attempt to confiscate those eagle feathers as they come by. I think the game wardens might need backup, however, like all the SWAT teams in the state of Wisconsin, the National Guard, and the 173rd Airborne Brigade.

I was in the Twin Cities when U.S. Senator Daniel Inouye was holding hearings about amending the Indian Religious Freedom Act. According to the senator, the purpose of the hearing was to protect Indian religious rights, including the right to own eagle feathers. Senator Inouye was presented with an eagle feather during the hearings. I heard President Clinton was given an eagle feather also. Do you suppose the game wardens would try to "monitor" the use of those feathers? I don't think so.

We are watching to see how this curious story unfolds. In the meantime, I went trolling for game wardens in Wisconsin. My eagle feather was prominently hanging from my rearview mirror. I didn't get a nibble. Maybe the game wardens were patrolling in the casino parking lots.

It is scary to know there are armed men about, acting under the color of their badges, confiscating eagle feathers.

In continuing to answer the Black Bear Casino employee who wanted to know what we want, I would say answers to the social problems that plague us. Racism, alcoholism, and poverty are just a few. I could quote a ricing basket filled with statistics about infant mortality, teen suicide, and dysfunctional families but I won't. They are problems but are not unique to us. Racism itself is not unique to us. It is part of the price we pay for living here, living in these times.

In spite of the obvious racism we live with, I suspect there are quite a few people who want to be Indian. I think so because of all the people who come up and tell me they are part Indian. I wish I had a roll of quarters for every time that has happened.

Whenever I hear that, I immediately wonder—which part? The right hand or the whole arm? The liver or spleen? Hearing that someone is part Indian is a never-ending source of humor for me. Some of us have white ancestors but we don't brag about it or run up and tell every white person we meet.

Perhaps it is our spirituality people are seeking after all. The rent-a-shamans who peddle ceremonies are one prime example. First, I wonder why they pick us and our ceremonies? I have never heard of a sham Shinto shaman, an imitation rabbi, or an infidel imam. Just us and the bogus sweat lodge, bogus sun dance, and other pretend ceremonies and activities.

One such activity was a class offered by a local arts organization. The two-day class was a repeat from the year before. We missed hearing about it the first time but this year we noticed it. The class was called Building a Medicine Drum.

I called the arts organization for more information. They sent me some background information about the presenters. Both appeared to be full-blooded white people. One listed his credentials as follows:

Member, Order of the Arrow Dance Team

First Place Winner, Order of the Arrow Indian Costume Contest

Cultural Tutor, teaching Native American students native crafts and spirituality in Michigan

Researcher, Native American arts and crafts in Arizona and Michigan

On the Rez, in the little village of Sawyer, we determined that this was a rent-a-shaman scam. We asked the arts organization if we could sit in and observe. We have had some experience with drums and drum building. We were told we couldn't because "it is uncomfortable for the participants."

The only other way in was to pay $135 like everyone else.

The arts organization had a change of heart and decided to drop the drum-making class. I think it was the threat of being called culture vultures that did it. Some elders in Sawyer were disappointed because they wanted to meet a real live rent-a-shaman.

When my wife and I were in Aberdeen, Scotland, we just missed meeting one. The rent-a-shaman stalking the land was calling himself Pretty Painted Arrow. He was selling sweat lodge ceremonies, pipe ceremonies, and vision quests.

Alas, there was a scandal reported in the newspapers. Pretty Painted Arrow left town with another man's wife. She must have liked the color of his Arrow, I surmised.

Our trails didn't cross, but with so many shamans about I expect to meet one any time now. The story about Pretty Painted Arrow is good for a laugh at any gathering of Shinnobs.

I have met many fine people who don't claim to be something they are not. They just live our values and respect our traditions. Those who respect our ways, our history, get my respect. That's what it boils down to, respect—mutual respect.

It is hard to get respect in the history books and museums that claim to represent our past.

One day we motored to the Fairlawn Museum in Superior, Wisconsin. It had been several years since we last saw Sitting Bull's doorknob and hinges from his cabin. In addition to the door parts, the museum has a collection of old photographs taken by David Francis Barry. They span the years 1874–1890. Most of the photographs were of the Lakota people. Someone gave the door parts to the photographer and the museum displayed them.

We wanted to see the door parts again but they were not to be found. They were not on display and we helped look in a storage closet for the missing door parts. While looking around, I found an old Ojibwe prayer book which was published in 1851. The prayer book also contained two four-leaf clovers, a lock of brown hair, and prayer cards. The seven-hundred-page book had a brown leather binding. It looked old. It was full of old words, old prayers.

I wondered if I could find a prayer in there to help me find Sitting Bull's doorknob.

I checked a couple of months later and the door parts were still missing. The Fairlawn Museum did get two dance shields back. They were recovered by the FBI in St. Louis, Missouri. The artifacts were stolen in 1978 and the museum received $30,500 for their loss. They used the money to repair the roof and to buy more David Francis Barry photographs.

Ownership of the dance shields passed to the insurance company when they were recovered. The insurance company donated them back to the Fairlawn Museum. Harold Gronquist, President of the Historical Society, said security has increased since the theft. He also said, "They're back where they belong."

No one thought to ask the Lakota people if they would be interested in getting the dance shields back.

Other items missing from the museum's collection include Sitting Bull's rifle and war shield, a Lakota ceremonial dress, and other war clubs. Meanwhile, I am left wondering if the FBI is involved in the case of the missing doorknob and hinges from Sitting Bull's cabin.

I learned more about museums at Todd County, Minnesota. "Stones and Bones" was the title of a display I came across in the historical (hysterical?) museum.

The bones were glued to a piece of plywood along with some stones. Crude ballpoint pen lettering identified the objects on the plywood. The stones were identified as petrified wood, iron ore, a meteorite, and an agate. Some stone arrowheads were glued to the plywood also. The bones were identified as "human" (Indian) on the label.

I am not a doctor but the bone looked like it came from someone's leg. One joint was still attached to the leg bone. There were several small fragments that looked the same in color and texture. I was shocked. I almost said, "Gramma, what did they do to you? Where is the rest of you?"

I asked curator Don Hayes if they had any more bones. He rummaged around under a table and brought out two yellow shoeboxes. He opened one and dug out a human skull. I didn't want to see any more. I asked if we could leave because I felt extremely uncomfortable standing there. We left to check the museum's records to see where the bones came from.

The Stones and Bones exhibit was donated to the museum by Leonard Markfelder of Staples, Minnesota. Between the years 1973–1978, he donated other objects to the museum also. Those objects included a rifle as well as a stuffed groundhog, falcon, osprey, and snapping turtle.

The curator said they were looking for a way to dispose of the bones but didn't know how. I gave them the telephone number of the Minnesota Indian Affairs Council.

A day later I asked if they had contacted anyone about the bones. They said they hadn't called anyone. Wilma Finseth of the Todd County Museum said they did have more information about the skull.

Her files showed the skull was part of a burial bundle found when a garage was being built in Long Prairie, Minnesota. Curator Finseth said the bones had been studied at St. Cloud State University and then returned to the museum. The burial bundle was found in 1957 or '58.

Later, at the museum, I noticed the leg bone was now chipped off the plywood. Its new home was a paper towel. Curator Finseth said the museum was still unable to contact anyone about the bones. Meanwhile, the two sets of bones remain locked in the museum. I left knowing I would be back to check on their progress.

A month later I learned that the museum had contacted an Anishinaabe, Earl Sargent, at Hamline University, St. Paul. To paraphrase Spike Lee, thank you Todd County Museum for finally doing the right thing. They will return the bones to the earth.

As long as people see us as barely human, nearly extinct relics not worthy of a proper burial, we have a problem. Racism could be defined as a serious image problem. In my lifetime, I have dedicated a lot of hours to changing the perception of us. I am one of the modern Anishinaabeg men, the contemporary Chippewa, the omnifarious Ojibwe, the savvy Shinnob. I'll tell you one thing we are not. We are not at the end of the trail.

Like most things that are overdone, the "End Of The Trail" has outlived its time. Just once, I would like to see what that Indian looked like at the beginning of the trail. Better yet, I would like to see the tired Indian with an international symbol of a red circle and a slash covering every representation of the "End Of The Trail." I think it is long past time to retire that particular image.

I see him slumped over his horse everywhere I go. The one I saw recently had mountains in the background, which made me think he was from a tribe west of us. I wondered what he would look like if he were a Shinnob? Would he be depicted draped over his parching kettle? Would he be hunched over in a sinking birch bark canoe?

Go to any powwow and you can find the tired Indian represented like Elvis on black velvet. The tired Indian is on paintings and prints; he can be seen in beaded belt buckles, earrings, and on clocks. He and his tired horse are everywhere. The Indian looks like he has a calcium deficiency or his backbone is made of rubber. The horse looks pretty bad too.

I wonder about the tired Indian. How did he get so beat-up looking? Was it a war, maybe a bad hunting trip? Were he and his horse on a long, dirty drunk? Then I wonder why we Shinnobs continue to embrace this image. Do we think he represents us? It certainly doesn't look like the finest memories of the old days.

Along with the tired Indian image, I'd like to shitcan all racist mascots. I came to realize it couldn't be ignored or forgiven. My son, Joseph, was watching the evening news on a local TV station. He heard the sports reporter say, "The '49ers scalped the Redskins."

Joseph, a sports jock, reacted quite quickly. He called the TV station to let them know he thought that was a racist thing to say. He was given the brush-off.

The next morning I went upstairs and called the news director of the station. He was surprised and said he is 1,000 percent against things like that. He said the sports reporter was new and it wouldn't happen again. The news director promised to work closer with the Indian community. He offered Joseph a tour of the studio as a way of making amends. My boy said he would rather play hoops someplace.

To paraphrase a quote about hockey, "we went to a protest and a Super Bowl broke out." We joined Shin-

nobs at the Peacemaker Center in Minneapolis. We were
part of a crowd that gathered to hear speeches from
leaders of AIM, the American Indian Movement, and
U.S. Senator Paul Wellstone.

It was a typical Minnesota January. There was wind,
windchill, and snow. In the crowd, someone was passing
out chemical hand-warmers. I heard one Shinnob tell
another one, "Don't eat that candy, it tastes funny."

They were just being Shinnobs, finding something to
joke about regardless of the situation.

My cousin, Rathide, suggested we go to a Saints' or
Padres' game dressed as Catholics. What a great idea, I
thought. Get thirty Shinnobs, put miters and vestments
on them. They could carry rosaries, let people kiss their
ring and wash their feet. Rathide also reminded me
when the Catholics first came, they had the Bible and we
had the land. Out of respect, we shut our eyes and got
down on our knees to pray with them. When we got up,
we had the Bible and they had the land. I decided not to
dress as a Catholic.

The sound of a drum drew us to the Hubert H.
Humphrey Metrodome. It was the site of the next part of
the protest against racism in sports. I ignored the white
people scalping football tickets on my way to the
protest. The Buffalo and Washington fans were greeted
by Shinnobs carrying anti-racist signs. The fans looked
at the signs and quickly looked away. We could almost
feel their eyes glaze over.

The protesters marched around the Metrodome. That
was a wise tactical move by the protest organizers. It
was too cold to stand around listening to speeches.
While marching around the Metrodome, I saw only one
real live redskin.

My grandson, Ezigaa, pointed him out to me. It was a drunken white man wearing shorts, paint, and feathers. The little he wore didn't protect him from the cold. His skin was burnished red by the wind. His beer belly was the same color as the paint on his face. He was a redneck and more. We thought we were lucky to have a white man honoring us by freezing his skin. We felt warm because we were striking a blow against racism. I guess after we left, they played a football game in the HHH Metrodome.

Names and labels are important. It made it easier to kill Vietnamese during the war if we called them gooks, dinks, or slopes. We didn't see them as human beings, they weren't fathers, brothers, or sons. They were just a label and that shows the power of labeling.

The *Minneapolis Star-Tribune* decided to quit using sports nicknames that were offensive to us.

Dominic Papatola, a critic from the Duluth newspaper, wrote that the Minneapolis newspaper was damaging its credibility by not printing offensive nicknames. He calls it quibbling about semantics. I think he is carrying on an academic argument with himself. I looked at racism in the media again after seeing his response. Some, like Papatola, would rather talk lofty concepts when they should be down in the gutter of reality.

It was reality when my son, Joseph, was shown the tomahawk chop by his white classmates. Of course, they waited until the teacher's back was turned. They were chopping away at his identity and self-esteem. That was racism learned directly from the sports teams. The chopping movement was used to deliver a brutal message of hate. The fact that it happened in Civics class made it worse, somehow.

It is fortunate that Papatola hasn't experienced racism on a daily basis. It makes it easier for him to stand on the outside and decide what is "politically correct." He echoes others when he says that education is the answer to racist nicknames.

We have protested racist nicknames at the World Series and Super Bowl games. Shinnobs were there to protest and educate fans about offensive nicknames. How much more educating do we have to do? Would yet another news release help?

Perhaps the Indian casinos could use their economic clout to educate people about offensive nicknames. The casinos could band together and buy World Series and Super Bowl ad time. They could use their thirty seconds to promote mutual respect instead of offensive nicknames. On the local level, Indian casinos could buy ad space from newspapers that don't print such names. Casino advertising money is a big hammer.

Offensive nicknames are just one of racism's ugly faces and changing such nicknames is the only remedy

Critic Papatola is one of the keepers of the status quo. I thought newspapers were supposed to educate and inform. By taking such a strong stand, the *Star-Tribune* is educating its readers to the reality of racist nicknames. It is informing readers that they won't be part of a business that says it is good business to demean a specific group of humans. Their efforts should be applauded, their actions emulated.

By not using racist nicknames, we move beyond merely being politically correct to showing mutual respect.

Fighting racism is a lifelong struggle for those who are affected by it. In the late 1800s, the policy of shooting Indians was pretty much over. We became U.S. citizens in 1924. In 1936, tribal governments were given constitutions and the right to govern themselves. In the '60s, we got civil rights. In the 1970s, we finally got religious freedom. Gambling came along in the 1980s. From shooting to gambling in just a few generations is quite a change.

But it has been a long trail. All of us want to make the trail easier for our children and grandchildren. It was a Chinese man, not a gook, who said the longest trail begins with a single step.

One step backward is the trend in this country to call those with light skin immigrants and those with dark skin refugees. I heard one U.S. government official say people were being sent back to their homeland because they were not political but economic refugees. Can we make that policy retroactive? Can we send someone back who came here for economic reasons? Maybe add something to the Statue of Liberty that says, "Give me your tired, your poor, your huddled masses yearning to be free, as long as they are the right color."

Racism is not easy to discuss. I've been called a racist myself. I write occasionally for area newspapers. Many places in my writings, I use the term "white man."

Someone who lives near the Rez wrote to accuse me of being a racist. I was going to ignore it but decided to explore the issue in my column. I tried to think of some alternatives to "white man." How about *gichimookomaan*, our word for the Americans encountered by our ancestors? In our language, it means big knife. When they first met us, these colonial Americans had swords and bayonets. But who would want to be known as a "big knifer"? What about Caucasian? Call them

Cauky for short. Maybe a term like European would
work, but I'm not sure if the pale-skinned Irish or Scots
ever wanted to be part of Europe at all. I got it, we'll call
you Invaderman.

I'm at a loss here but am taking suggestions.

To turn the tables, during the celebrations honoring
Christopher Columbus, I decided to do something about
terms and labels.

For five hundred years we have been called something we're not. It started with Columbus, then continued with the Puritans and Cotton Mather. Along the
way, the United States government started using the
term to describe us. Hollywood films and other forms of
mass media have perpetuated the use of the word Indian. It has been so common, we have internalized it. We
have heard it so much, we began to think we are Indian.

I'm not Indian, I'm Anishinaabe.

Columbus was just the point man for the invasion of
this hemisphere. A way of life that was ecologically
sound was transformed. We now exist in a poisoned,
polluted place. Christianity and the lust for gold have
replaced respect for the land, air, and water.

How do you insult a Shinnob?

Call him or her a Columbus lover.

As my way of de-celebrating the events marking the
500th anniversary of Columbus's arrival in this hemisphere, I vowed to quit using the word Indian. It would
not cross my lips for one year. Instead of saying the
word, I would use silence. Instead of writing the word

out, I would use dashes. In anticipation of the anniversary, I banished the word from my working vocabulary on October 12, 1991.

According to the reference books, we are called Indians because Columbus didn't know he had stumbled onto a new continent. He was originally looking for a sea route to India and China.

Thinking that he had made it to India, he called the people he met _____. He liked some of these people so much he took some back to Europe as slaves. He called his slaves _____.

We have been using this word so much, we have overdone it. In the _____ newspapers that carry my column, I found 333 uses of the word in *The Circle. News From* _____ *Country* used it 342 times in 32 pages. In the *Ojibwe News,* I found it was used 417 times in 12 pages. In my own Fond du Lac Follies, I found 19 examples of the word in the past year.

Dropping the word _____ was fun. I called that Hoosier state _____a, its capital was _____apolis. When talking about the American _____ Movement, I used silence in the middle. When I went to the federal building, I was talking to bureaucrats from the Bureau of _____ Affairs.

There were enough examples to keep it interesting. The _____ Health Service, the National _____ Gaming Act, the Cleveland _____ baseball team. The road sign at the edge of the Rez should read: THE FOND DU LAC _____ RESERVATION. My kids were still playing, only now they were playing Cowboys and _____.

Out of hundreds of thousands of words in the English language, I could afford to give that one a small vacation. I realized that the word is a permanent part of the

English language but giving it up for one year was my way of de-celebrating Columbus.

I foolishly promised my son, Joseph, a dollar every time I slipped up and used the word. At the end of that year, I had given him $383 for my mistakes. My boy learned the power of words and labels. That was a small price to pay for him to learn such a big thing. Indian is no longer a part of his vocabulary either. He asks tribal people what they would like to be called. My son wants me to banish another word from my vocabulary. He likes making money from my mistakes.

At the end of my column, the Fond du Lac Follies, I usually remind readers that I speak for no one but myself, not the Fond du Lac Reservation people; the Reservation Business Committee; the newspapers that carry the column; my neighbors; my cousin Rathide; my cousins and friends: Butch, Punkin, Chuck, Pea, Sam, Meat, and the rest; the state of Minnesota; the county of Carlton; the inventor of duct tape; Eye of Newt Ging-RICH; or my wife Patricia.

The questions I ask and the answers I find interest and satisfy me. I hope to find the answers to racism somewhere along the trail. It has been a long trail and we're not at the end of it. We're not even beginning to slump in our canoes.

Politics

....

OBABAAMIZIWINIWA

FOR CENTURIES NOW, we have struggled to maintain our space, our societies, our identity, and spirituality. On this continent there are over five hundred tribes of native people. We are one of them. We must like governments because we have another layer, one more than the average U.S. citizen. In addition to the federal, state, and county governments that oversee almost all parts of our lives, we have a form of tribal government.

We elect our leaders every four years and it has been said they sometimes elect themselves. We don't have chiefs anymore, we have a chairman, a secretary/treasurer, and precinct representatives. We use Bob's Rules, *Robert's Rules of Order,* to conduct our tribal business. Our sixty-year experiment in representative democracy is continuing.

Our formal, federal name is the Fond du Lac Band of Lake Superior Chippewa. We are governed by a constitution written by the Bureau of Indian Affairs in the 1930s. Our chairman and secretary/treasurer also sit on the Tribal Executive Committee of the Minnesota Chippewa Tribe. This federal corporation administers our affairs on the tribal level. It was also established in the 1930s. The TEC consists of members from six reservations: Fond du Lac, Grand Portage, Bois Forte, Leech Lake, Mille Lacs, and White Earth.

Our constitution is similar to the U.S. Constitution with one major exception. There is no separation of powers and the Reservation Business Committee is our whole government. This fatal flaw in our constitution allows the RBC almost unlimited power. The RBC has the final say on any reservation job. They decide who lives here through the housing program. The RBC runs the casinos. Here is how it works:

An application is made by Fond du Lac Management, Inc., for a "gaming" license to operate two casinos. The application and letterhead lists the Board of Directors.

Hey, wait a minute. These are the same five men who sit as RBC members. Did they really ask themselves for a license?

I wasn't there but I would surmise they sat on one side of the table to present the application. Then they would stand up, walk around the table, becoming RBC members on the way. Want to guess how the vote went on that application?

This has been happening since the ordinance was passed by the RBC in 1993. It ain't pretty but it is what passes for democracy on the Fond du Lac Reservation.

What is a common phrase heard around the RBC?

They can't do that, can they?

For example, a few years back there was an allegation of voter fraud in one of our tribal elections. A candidate for one of the offices thought an incumbent broke election laws to get re-elected.

Let's see if we can follow the twisted logic used by the tribal government in their fight to protest the protest of the election.

June 9, an election is held on the Fond du Lac Reservation.

June 10, the election results are certified by the Election Board appointed by the RBC.

June 15, Tribal Court Judge Dee Fairbanks issues the Rules Governing Election Protests.

June 17, one candidate files an election protest.

June 19, the Election Board holds a pre-hearing on the protest. They move to dismiss the protest.

June 29, Judge Fairbanks is directed by Chip Wadena, President of the Minnesota Chippewa Tribe, to dismiss the protest.

July 8, Judge Fairbanks decides to proceed with the protest hearing.

July 14, Chip Wadena again directs Judge Fairbanks not to hold the protest hearing.

The legal wrangling goes on all summer.

August 14, Judge Fairbanks schedules a hearing for August 24.

August 24, Judge Fairbanks is fired by the RBC. The protest is once again relegated to legal limbo. The incumbent votes to keep himself in office.

In a news release about the firing of the judge, the RBC said the judge's actions posed a "threat to the integrity of the election process and the rule of law on the Fond du Lac Reservation."

In a response to the RBC, former judge Fairbanks said, "They're jeopardizing sovereignty by doing this. When we violate due process and tribal governments start stomping on the rights of individuals whose rights they should be protecting, I get very worried. I wouldn't be very proud of myself right now if I were a Fond du Lac elected official."

In a public letter, Fairbanks told the RBC that it had "made a mockery of our Tribal Court System. . . . It is clear that you will allow only a puppet court to work for you. I can only hope that you will seriously consider the repercussions beyond your own self interests and allow your court system and your laws to work."

Without a judge, our tribal court was adrift, there in name only. Since we didn't have one, the RBC had to buy us a new one. Rumors were flying on the moccasin telegraph (the Rez gossip network) about who the new judge would be. Two names mentioned most frequently were Kurt Blue Dog, an attorney from another Reservation, and the RBC's man, Dennis Peterson, their attorney.

Peterson usually acts as the prosecutor. Let us see what could happen if the RBC appointed him as judge of the tribal court.

There might be a silver lining in this judicial dark cloud. The last two judges we had were fired by the RBC. Judge Patrick O'Brien was fired for his opposition to the 1854 Treaty sale. Judge Fairbanks was found guilty of following her conscience. Maybe Peterson will get himself fired?

Peterson in a robe? Let us see what might happen if he tries to do both jobs.

Say, for example, a Shinnob is dragged into court for

a game violation. Peterson, as prosecutor, would bring the charges.

I can see it now. The Rez prosecutor comes into the courtroom. I see that he is hopping. His heels are together, arms held at chest level, his fingers are pointing down as he hops to the prosecutor's table. He opens his leather pouch and takes out his papers. When he is done, he smiles up at the judge's bench.

He leaps to his feet and hops up to the bench. When he removes his coat to put on the robe, I see he is wearing a gavel in a holster on his hip, both hips. He buttons the robe and sits down. On his way down, he does a cross-body draw and comes up with a gavel. He spins it a couple of times before pounding on the bench. When he crosses his legs, I spot a smaller gavel in an ankle holster. He smiles at the prosecutor's table and tells him to bring in the guilty Shinnob so the trial can proceed. The fish fuzz, game wardens, open the door and yell at the Shinnob, who is outside having a last smoke. He refuses their offer of a blindfold and walks into the courtroom. The judge, using his gavel, points at the defense table. The Shinnob sits down and looks around. He doesn't see any of his relatives in the room, just an Australian travel poster hanging on the wall. He looks out the window.

The Shinnob is sitting alone at the defense table . . .

The judge asks the prosecutor if he would like to make an opening statement. Peterson jumps up, holsters the gavel, and removes the robe. He takes one mighty bound to the prosecutor's table. Once there, he faces the judge's bench and begins to lay out the case he will be prosecuting.

At one point in the opening statement, Peterson objects to one of his own statements. He looks to the bench for a ruling. Peterson stops, hops to the bench to rule on the objection.

As judge, Peterson always sustains prosecutor Peterson's objections. The courtroom is silent as the judge makes his ruling. Peterson holsters the gavel, removes the robe, and bounds back to the prosecutor's table.

Peterson thanks the judge for the profound, very profound ruling. Robe time again as Peterson hops back to the bench to thank the prosecutor. Once again, back to the prosecutor's table for Peterson who continues to argue his case.

Once, when the Shinnob laughs at something Peterson says, the prosecutor hops quickly to the bench. He jams the robe on, twirls the gavel, and warns the Shinnob that if there are any further outbursts, he will clear the courtroom. The judge stares hard at the guilty Shinnob. He then removes the robe. We notice he is getting real good at that robe business.

While Peterson argues, we have time to see he is still wearing the bruise he got on his face when he was arguing a fine point of Indian law with a Shinnob on another Reservation.

Finally when Peterson is done arguing, he hops up to the bench and puts the robe on. Peterson sits there in all his majesty, surveying his, that's right, his courtroom.

The Shinnob continues gazing out the window. We are all waiting for the ruling. The game wardens are waiting as is the court clerk. The tension in the room could be cut with a chainsaw.

Finally Judge Peterson decides the guilty Shinnob is guilty. He pronounces a fine and asks if there is any further business for the court. It is quite a long time before we see Peterson begin to remove the robe. He takes it off slowly, seeming to fondle the material between his thumb and fingers. He holsters both gavels and springs back to the table where prosecutor Peterson thanks the judge for his even-handed administration of justice. Robe time again as he acknowledges the prosecutor's words. The judge pounds his gavel on the bench to close the session. It sounds so good, he draws his backup gavel and does a two-handed chop. He twirls, then holsters the hip gavels and draws the small one from the ankle holster, pounds, then declares court is over for the day. Peterson takes the robe off for the last time and leisurely hops back to the prosecutor's table. Once at the table, he puts his papers in his pouch. The judge and the prosecutor hop out of the courtroom together. Peterson has both paws held in front of his chest.

It's official, we have a kangaroo court at Fond du Lac. While this may have been speculation, it is scary because it could really happen. As the guilty Shinnob might say, there's law and order and just us.

I know the history of the Anishinaabeg. My ancestors fought few bloody battles with the invaders. Instead, small fights were waged in the woods, on the lakes, and everywhere the settlers came to claim lands we once used. No last stands took place, no one marched us to another area. Our women and children were not murdered by the U.S. Cavalry during the brutal winters. We won the battle of Sugar Point, Anishinaabeg warriors drove off the troops from Fort Snelling. We lost almost everything else in the paper wars that followed contact with the white people.

Our history is one of fur traders, missionaries, forts, Reservations, treaties, and disappearing land. It is also one of cultural genocide as the white man tried to make us over in his image.

How did Shinnobs survive the Great Depression?

I didn't know it was over.

We don't even have the same holidays. Instead of Columbus Day, we call it a Day of Mourning, with tongue in cheek, of course. I know we can't change the past so we just enjoy the present with hopes for the future of the Anishinaabeg. We eat wild rice like the Shinnobs were doing hundreds of years ago when Columbus landed.

Do you celebrate Thanksgiving?

Yah, but it's getting harder to find Pilgrims.

Most people know who they are because of their parents and grandparents. Some might even know who their great-grandparents are. In our family oral history, I can tell you who my relatives are going back to about 1740, when Mikinaak, my great-great-great-great-great-great grandfather, was living his life here with the seasons. I know the names and stories of the people that came after him. I teach my children so they will have something to teach their children.

The Anishinaabeg had a system of clans and bands to tell one another apart until the United States government decided all indigenous people needed to be enrolled. They counted heads, marked their maps, and waited for the math to work against us.

With the exception of Red Lake, Minnesota reservations were subdivided during the Dawes Allotment Act period in the 1880s. All adult Shinnobs were given title to eighty acres of their own land. After they got their land allotments, there was land that was unalloted. This land was declared surplus and thrown open to white settlers making the word Reservation a lie. The land assigned to the Shinnobs became subject to taxation after a period of years. Most of the people lost their allotments to tax forfeiture and Minnesota became a big landowner on the Reservation. Today, out of the 100,000 acres specified in the Treaty of 1854, we own about 22,000 acres. We have lost four-fifths of our land base since the treaty was signed.

Why were the treaties etched on real thin glass?

Easier to break, of course.

The land base was shattered and the cultural genocide continued with the policies of assimilation, relocation, and termination. Most of the land and the language were lost but the Anishinaabe were still here, confident in their identity, looking forward to each day the Creator gives. Now our language speakers are teaching the language again and the RBC is rebuilding the land base using gambling gold.

But, like most governments, the Reservation Business Committee is not always wise. In 1988, they wanted to sell our 1854 Treaty rights to the state of Minnesota. The rights to hunt, fish, and gather in the ceded territory were reserved by the Anishinaabe when they signed the documents. The ceded territory includes parts of three states: Minnesota, Wisconsin, and Michigan.

The old stories say the treaties are still valid and the 1993 Voight case in Wisconsin reaffirmed the rights of the Anishinaabe to hunt, fish, and gather there.

The RBC surprised us when they told us they had been negotiating for months with the state over our treaty rights. The negotiations were secret because, as the then-chairman told me, "We don't want to show our hand."

At first I wondered, why the state? We signed the treaties with the federal government. Minnesota didn't exist until some four years after the 1854 Treaty was signed.

Then I remembered. For many years, the state has been hunting Shinnobs who were using their treaty rights to hunt, fish, and gather. They have been jailed, their food's been confiscated, and they've had to pay fines for violations of state game laws.

At first it was confusing. According to the state, we don't have treaty rights but if we do have them, the state will give us $1.85 million if we don't use them.

The arrogance of the RBC was shown when the chairman said, "You voted for us. We'll make these decisions for you."

In the informational meetings that followed, we were assured that this was not a treaty sale. The proposed agreement to sell the rights didn't actually buy the treaty, just the right to use it. There was no difference between selling the treaty and not being able to use it, I thought.

In the meetings, we learned the right to collect for past damages was bargained away early in the negotiations. One hundred thirty-four years of wrongs erased with the stroke of a pen, I thought. We were informed by the RBC that we didn't have a right to vote on such an issue.

In the tribal form of government we only have two recourses for wrongs committed against us. One is the election process, which is flawed because the RBC appoints the election board which oversees the elections. The second is to petition for a referendum. We chose the second.

We gathered signatures for a petition. Once we had enough we turned it in to the secretary/treasurer. He looked at it and threw it out because we didn't follow the procedures. This is the first time we ever tried it and we didn't know there were procedures to follow. We asked for the guidelines for a referendum.

With guidelines in hand, we petitioned again for a referendum. We were stalled at every turn but did gather enough signatures. The people voted down the treaty sale.

We didn't know it, but the agreement had already been signed by the time we heard about it so the vote was meaningless. I think the RBC was blinded by the money that was offered by the state. I guess 1.85 million dollars buys a lot of conscience.

When we finally did get a copy of the agreement and studied it, we came to the conclusion that the agreement makes a mockery of our sovereignty. Even the tone of the document was condescending: "the state will . . . ," "the state shall . . . ," "the Indians may . . ."

As written, the agreement gives the state the right to oversee our tribal courts. It also says the state has the right to oversee the enforcement of our Conservation

Code. The document says we are a sovereign nation as long as the state approves, making a lie of the word sovereign.

So the treaty was sold. Grand Portage Reservation members got fifteen hundred dollars for their treaty rights; here at Fond du Lac we got a meaningless referendum and Bois Forte Reservation members didn't even get that.

After the information meetings, the Shinnobs of Fond du Lac were not satisfied with the information presented, the reasons given for selling the treaty, and why it all happened so quickly. We knew from the old stories that three thousand to four thousand Shinnobs gathered when it was time to sign the original document. We didn't think five people of the RBC should have that much power to decide something so important.

People gathered at the community center in Sawyer to talk about treaties. The people who came were of the same mind—treaties should not be sold. Most people felt the treaties are for us to use while we are here but ultimately the rights belong to the generations to come.

After the people's meeting in Sawyer, we formed a group to resist any further losses of our treaty rights. Like any group, we decided we needed a name to identify ourselves. We were already labeled dissidents by our Rez government.

At first, we thought of something simple and direct. Someone suggested calling ourselves Fonjalackers Against Treaty Selling. It met our needs for an identity but we had to shitcan it because someone pointed out that the initials spelled the word FATS. Since there already was a Minnesota Fats who played pool, we decided to modify our name. We tinkered with it and came up with Fonjalackers Against Selling Treaties. It spelled FAST, a little better, a little zippier but still not quite right. That is when we decided on ALF, the Anishinaabe Liberation Front. It was almost sinister sounding, bringing to mind some of the liberation organizations of the 1960s.

We became ALF for a couple of reasons. We knew we would be of interest to the media. We wanted to force them to use the word Anishinaabe, our name for ourselves. The second reason is a lot of us used to like that little orange creature on a TV sitcom named Alf.

ALF members lobbied the state legislators in the halls and in the hearings. We were there to convince them not to appropriate the money for the treaty buyout. They listened politely but voted to spend the money anyway.

We also testified in federal court about the proposed treaty sale. We thought we were lucky to be heard in that venue, but once again the deal was cut, dried, and wrapped before we got there. We couldn't convince the judge that the people's vote should have a bearing on the matter of a treaty sale.

ALF members became media darlings as we tried to explain our side of the issue. All of our efforts were fruitless because it was a done deal.

Fond du Lac Band members lost the right to hunt, fish, and gather in the ceded territory for one year. The next year, the tribal government wanted to sell the rights again. Since we had already voted the treaty sale down, it was necessary for us to vote again. We took the extraordinary step of voting in a nonelection year. I think our constitution was bent to allow an unscheduled vote.

The people of the Rez voted down the treaty sale again. Grand Portage and Bois Forte still remain in the agreement. Here at Fond du Lac, we once again have our rights guaranteed in the Treaty of 1854.

The band leaders who sold the treaty are no longer in office and the lawyers who advised them are no longer working for Fond du Lac.

ALF was right, we do have treaty rights. According to Judge Richard Kyle, Fond du Lac continues to possess the right to hunt, fish, and gather in the ceded territory of the 1837 and 1854 Treaties. The March 18, 1996, ruling resolves the Phase l issues about the existence of Fond du Lac's treaty rights. Phase ll will determine the allocation of natural resources between FDL band members and non-band members (Minnesota citizens).

The ruling by Judge Kyle gave me a chance to reflect on the fish wars. Spearing fish bothers most of the anti-treaty groups that have festered and grown since the Voight decision in Wisconsin. One man, Larry Peterson, was talking the loudest in his opposition to treaty rights. He was a member and spokesman for PARR, Protect America's Rights and Resources.

We went to a PARR meeting. Shinnobs heard about the meeting and decided to attend. We wanted a chance to see, up close, those with necks of red.

We formed a two-car convoy and motored to the meeting. It was held at the Town of Superior Hall. As we drove down dark Highway 35, the streetlights got farther and farther apart. We found the hall and locked our cars in the dim parking lot.

Inside, Mr. PARR himself, Larry Peterson, was greeting those who were walking in. He reminded me of a preacher welcoming the faithful. He went out of his way to be friendly to the Shinnobs.

The room was large and well lit. Folding chairs were set up with an aisle of about six feet between the two sections. PARR newspapers were displayed on a side table. The head table was under the flags of the Rotary Club, the Lions Club, and the stars and stripes of the United States.

A man, later introduced as Wayne Powers, was sitting at the head table. When the people coming in sat at the back of the hall, like church, Powers said, "C'mon up front. We don't have our white sheets on tonight. Move up front, we don't bite."

Larry Peterson went to the front of the hall to promptly open the meeting. Apparently PARR doesn't run on Indian time (defined as things happen when they're supposed to).

Peterson is a tall, thin, white man. He waves his skinny fingers around as he talks. He wore Kmart kind of clothes, holding up his pants with a belt with a turquoise buckle. He seemed at ease, as if preaching to the converted. About fifty people were listening to his words. The right-wing types sat on the right side of the aisle, the Shinnobs sat on the left.

Larry filled the hall with propaganda. He gave PARR's version of history, PARR's interpretation of federal court decisions. Peterson used fear and scare tactics. The center aisle seemed to grow wider as he talked. We laughed and joked in Ojibwe at some of his bald-faced lies. He identified all those responsible for the treaty "problem."

Among those blamed were the liberal judges of the federal court, the cops with their dogs, the paper mills for sitting back, the media, U.S. Senator Inouye, and Wisconsin Governor Tommy Thompson.

The Chippewa were blamed for depleting the resources, for the potential harm to tourism, loss of timber, clouded land titles, and declining property values. I was glad he didn't blame us for starting the Civil War or running the Exxon *Valdez* aground, although I expected him to.

Larry introduced Wayne Powers, PARR member. Powers, who talked earlier about white sheets, claims to be one-eighth Cherokee. He said his fight is not with the Chippewa, but with the federal government. He does not favor abrogating the treaties, just modifying to bring them up to modern times. He didn't explain how wearing white sheets would help.

There was a stir in the hall when the local TV news crews arrived. Apparently the electronic media does run on Indian time. Peterson went out to face the lights and cameras.

While Peterson was gone, Powers continued shoveling out propaganda and half-truths.

Peterson came back and resumed placing blame for the "treaty problem." He said one part of the "problem" is the person who carries the fake Indian head on a spear at the boat landing demonstrations,

"It's crap, it's bullshit. We will find out if that person is a member of PARR. He represents right-wing idiots."

In response to a question on what was a greater threat to the resources, Indians or pollution, Peterson replied, "Treaties are the worst form of pollution."

Peterson concluded the meeting by telling the right half of the hall that PARR needs grassroots volunteers. He asked them to join and buy memberships, T-shirts, jackets, and hats.

The right half of the hall got up to sign up. It is assumed that PARR member Wayne Powers will tell them when and where to wear the white sheets.

We didn't join, just left and drove down the dark highway to the lights of Duluth and Superior. I felt like I had seen enough of PARR and its methods.

While PARR was holding meetings, we were using our 1854 Treaty rights. Shinnobs from Fond du Lac have been using spears to get food. Some people opposed to spearing say we should do it like it was done in treaty signing times. Go back to the birch bark canoe and flaming torch. Why should we be stuck in the last century, I wondered? Yah, right. I'll go back to a birch bark canoe when you go back to a horse and buggy. Anishinaabe are alive today because we have changed and evolved.

When I spearfish, I use a steel spear. My spearing regalia consists of the following: an aluminum canoe, two paddles, two personal floatation devices, a car battery, wire, a motorcycle helmet and headlight, sometimes a file to keep things sharp. Finally, about three yards of gray duct tape to hold everything together.

One April, we went looking for the wily walleye.

We entered into the food gathering in a spiritual mood. We smudged and offered tobacco before we left. The Shinnobs wanted to think good thoughts when we were out on the lake. It felt good to be doing what Anishinaabeg have done down through the years.

The loons woke up when we got to the lake. They welcomed us with their songs. Once out on the lake, we just stopped and listened. It was quiet, except for the far off sound of trucks and trains.

Patchy, drifting fog surrounded us as we paddled along. The birds were sleeping in the trees. We woke four blue herons but a kingfisher wouldn't wake up. He was sleeping so deeply, he should have been snoring. A beaver came swimming up, apparently wanted to see what was going on with this light business. Mr. Muskrat showed us his hind end as he dove in front of the canoe. Under the water, bullheads and suckers went by like they knew we were only after walleye.

The walleye were easy to see, their eyes reflect the light. We saw some and speared them.

When we got back to the landing, the owls wanted to know who was out spearing. We took the fish home and shared them among our families.

People ask how many walleye did we get? We usually say, "Enough for a Shinnob, not enough for a Chimmook." (Rez slang: Shinnob=Indian, Chimmook=white man.)

We had been spearing for a while before the tribal government heard about it. The Reservation Business Committee did what they usually do, they held a meeting.

At the meeting, Chairman Peacock told the spearers "they would be thrown to the wolves."

Fond du Lac couldn't protect them if they were arrested by Minnesota game wardens. The reason was because we had a verbal agreement with the state. We reminded the chairman that verbal agreements are not worth the paper they are written on.

Chairman Peacock offered to give us fish if we stayed on the reservation. He told us he could get walleye from the state Department of Natural Resources. We told him we wouldn't accept two million dollars for treaty rights, why did he think we would accept a few fish, fish that we already owned under the treaty?

Another meeting produced a permit for spearers to gather food for a ceremony. Permit #001 was issued to Shinnobs from Fond du Lac.

The first night of permit spearing was uneventful except for the twelve gunshots heard by the spearers. The game wardens watching the spearers didn't hear the shots. The Shinnobs saw muzzle flashes, the game wardens saw someone with a flashlight. The Shinnobs wondered about the wisdom of bringing a spear to a gunfight.

The second night of permit spearing was more interesting. There were fifteen protesters at the boat landing. One of them wore a ski mask, reminded me of the massacre of the Israeli athletes at the Munich Olympics in 1972. When I carried my canoe to the lake, he said, "God damned Indians didn't have aluminum canoes one hundred years ago!"

"God damned Indians had treaty rights one hundred years ago, though," I replied.

The protesters were balanced by the fifteen trained witnesses. About fifteen law enforcement officers watched the two groups, protesters, and witnesses. The lights of a TV camera crew added to the ambiance of the dark boat landing.

The spearers went out looking for fish. They didn't see anything worth eating, only the usual assortment of beer cans. The Shinnobs found a huge wooden door floating in the lake. The spearers didn't spear any fish that night.

Chairman Peacock revoked the permit to spear because he said the ceremony was turning into a circus.
The spearers thought the chairman knew more about
circuses than ceremonies.

Shinnobs continued looking for fish in the ceded territory. They did it without a permit.

A couple days after the circus/ceremony, the RBC had
another meeting and decided to allow spearfishing for
any members of the Lake Superior Chippewa Bands
that had signed the Treaties of 1837, 1842, and 1854.
This permission included Shinnobs who live in Michigan
and Wisconsin.

After checking with their in-house legal counsel, the
RBC decided they couldn't give that kind of blanket permission. The RBC could only protect Shinnobs from
Fond du Lac. The Reservation Business Committee also
decided permits were no longer needed. All the spearers
had to do was let the game wardens know which lake
they would be using in the ceded territory.

Shinnob spearers continued looking for walleye until
then Governor Perpich and other Minnesota citizens
opened the regular state fishing season. Along the way
we met with members of the media. They seemed to
want a confrontational story. We told them what the
bottom of the lakes looked like but they were not interested in that story.

The elders from the village of Sawyer ate a walleye
dinner thanks to the spearers. The fish came from the
lakes in the ceded territory.

The Shinnob spearers from Fond du Lac thanked the
Creator for the fish; the game wardens, deputies, and
rescue squad for protection; the witnesses for their time
and courage; the protesters for their simple-minded op-

position; and all Shinnobs who supported the spearer's actions. The spearers especially thanked the Reservation Business Committee for their firm No, Yes, No, Yes, Maybe decision to allow spearing in the ceded territory.

PARR treaty protesters were still around. One showed up in an alternative newspaper in the Twin Cities. An issue of *City Pages* had one on the front page. He was giving a clenched fist salute; his hat read, "Save a wall-eye—spear a Indian."

Someone should have taken him to school before they took him out to the boat landing. Say it right fella, after all, it's your language. Say, "Save a walleye—spear *an* Indian."

As Shinnobs, we know the treaties have been under attack since the ink dried on the damn things. One of the things I have learned is to teach my children that their turn is coming. They will certainly have to use and protect their treaty rights. They might have to protect them from their own government.

Sometimes the tribal government stands on the sidelines when Shinnobs choose to exercise their treaty rights. It started innocently enough.

Walt Bresette, Red Cliff author, entrepreneur, and an all-around activist Shinnob started it when he invaded the Duluth, Minnesota, retail market. He opened a branch of the Buffalo Bay Trading Post at the Miller Hill Mall. Walt calls it shock retailing. He said the reactions to his opening range from "What are they doing in our mall?" to pleasant surprise. Walt says his business motto is, "Sell trinkets, not treaties." The store has pow-wow tapes, "I will snag no more forever" T-shirts, books, and Shinnob-made art in addition to the trinkets.

Walt caught the Christmas craziness wave just right

and described sales as brisk. He was doing well enough to buy art from local Shinnobs.

I've mentioned Esther Nahganub of Sawyer, who makes dreamcatchers and brings them to the mall to sell. She gets the feathers for her designs from road-killed birds and uses other natural materials in her dreamcatchers.

Walt displayed the dreamcatchers which contained feathers from a goose, a crow, and a hawk.

The trouble began in the form of Agent Duncan, a federal officer. While on routine patrol in the Miller Hill Mall, officer Duncan observed a violation of the Federal Migratory Bird Act.

He called for back-up and three Duluth Police officers, two mall security officers, and two Fond du Lac game wardens arrived to assist him. I counted six guns on the scene who were there to help Agent Duncan enforce provisions of the Migratory Bird Act.

Walt, Esther, and I were the only Shinnobs in the store. There were a couple of civilians playing the parts of customers.

Agent Duncan said he was there to confiscate the objects containing feathers. Walt Bresette told the federal officer he couldn't do that. The standoff began.

The civilians continued walking in and out of the store. Walt was still ringing on the cash register as the tense standoff dragged on.

After about three hours, Agent Duncan began stacking up all artwork that contained feathers. When he was done, he returned one object because it contained turkey feathers. He used a green garbage bag to carry the confiscated items. While this was going on, Esther tried to educate Agent Duncan about treaty rights in the ceded territory. When she tried to talk to the Reservation wardens, they just told her they were ashamed of her.

Agent Duncan told Walt he would have to appear in court in St. Paul. He gave Walt a receipt for the art objects and left the store with the confiscated items. The back-up officers stood around for a while then left.

Walt and Esther got lawyers to defend them against the federal government. We had a poet's/musician's benefit in Duluth to help raise money for their lawyers. Esther asked the Fond du Lac RBC for help in defending her case. The RBC turned her down, no money, no assistance in the treaty rights case. Both Walt and Esther were informed that if they paid a $500 fine, the feds would leave them alone.

We motored to St. Paul for the hearing in the federal court building. We went inside and listened to the testimony. Agent Duncan testified that it is legal to use goose feathers in fishing lures but not dreamcatchers; he further testified that it is legal to use them for pillows and vests but not dreamcatchers.

The defense attorney asked Agent Duncan if it would be legal to hang fishing lures from dreamcatchers, but the federal judge wouldn't allow that line of questioning. Briefs were filed by both sides and the judge said he would announce his decision.

We waited and the judge came out with an order that said we do have individual rights to use the treaty. Agent Duncan returned the dreamcatchers to Walt. That is when Walt offered to sell the dreamcatchers to Agent Duncan. He didn't buy but we felt like we had won a small battle in the treaty rights wars.

The 1854 Treaty rights issue went from a fast boil to a slow simmer. The 1837 Treaty was now beginning to heat up. The state of Minnesota wanted to buy treaty rights from the Mille Lacs people. They had informational meetings in the area affected by the treaty sale. In April of 1993, I attended hearings about the treaty sale. They were held in that big building with the four gold horses on the front, the state capital.

Marv Manypenny of White Earth was sitting at the witness table when I arrived. When he introduced himself to the state senators, he gave his name and tribe.

Marv took time out from his testimony to instruct the chairman of the subcommittee exactly how to say Anishinaabe.

I thought about that. Here we have important decisions being made and one of the key parties doesn't know how to say the name of the people he is dealing with. For our part, we know how to say Caucasian, white guy, American, Chimmook, senator, Republican, Democrat, and so on.

The legislators listened politely until Marv was done testifying.

Later, State Senator Lessard (can you say Anishinaabe?) said the 1837 Treaty sale legislation would not come out of his subcommittee to the full senate. As this is being written, the treaty sale might not go through. But then again, it might. Who knows?

Here at Fond du Lac, we know we signed the 1837 Treaty as did many other bands of the Lake Superior Chippewa. We're still not selling.

We were talking about the Mille Lacs treaty sale though. Shinnobs from Minnesota, Wisconsin, and Michigan gathered to talk about the latest attack on treaty rights. We wondered why the Mille Lacs people would sell the treaty?

ALF was reborn. We decided to use spears and nets to

gather fish from the ceded territory of the 1837 Treaty. ALF told the whole world we were going spearing at Mille Lacs to use our treaty rights. We met with the local sheriff and told him of our plans for a nonviolent protest of treaty selling. We told him where we would be spearing and netting.

The Shinnobs met at the East Lake Community Center. We were joined by the witnesses who came to show support for the Shinnobs. (These are folks from off the Rez who support our causes.) The media began arriving.

Dave Aubid from the Rice Lake band welcomed everyone to the East Lake Community Center. He brought out his drum and invited people to sing with him. My son, Jim, went in to sing. The sound of the drum brought people into a circle. The heartbeat of the drum and the power of the songs made us forget the media. It was hard to do, however.

At one point there were five TV satellite trucks parked on the gravel road in front of the community center. One Shinnob came out of the center, looked around, and asked if someone was going to launch a space shuttle. There were more microphones than spears at the gathering.

The center's kitchen was used to feed the multitudes that came to talk and use the 1837 Treaty. It was a good feast. The witnesses brought their food to the culturally diverse meal. Spinach-wrapped rice met frybread and deer meat. The fresh walleye was the centerpiece of the feast. No one questioned where the fish came from, they just ate it.

After the feast, the spearers met in an old school bus to talk strategy and tactics. While waiting for the dark we watched the sky. It had been half raining all day but the sky began to clear. A reporter with a pad and tape recorder wanted to know why we were not going spearing. A Shinnob told her we usually like to wait for dark, it makes things easier to see.

After we had our convoy of sixty cars and trucks together, we went to the planned primary site to spear. My son, Jim, and I were going out together. A witness named Chris LaForge came with us to observe from the shore of the lake. My car carried a canoe, a spear, and a light. We had personal floatation devices along because we didn't want to violate the state law that mandates the use of life jackets.

We followed Dave Aubid to Agate Bay on the east shore of Mille Lacs Lake. Our two cars pulled off the road to wait for the rest of the convoy. Just after we got out of the car, a shot was heard. I demonstrated my turtle reflex when I heard the gunfire. It sounded like a shotgun, maybe a .20 gauge We didn't hear any rounds going by but we did drift over and stand behind the engine block of our cars.

We notified the game wardens about the gunfire. They, in turn, notified the local sheriff who came to the scene. It became a law enforcement matter and we decided to go to our alternate site to spear. Once again, we questioned the wisdom of bringing a spear to a gunfight.

We drove south to Cedar Creek and took the canoe off the car and launched the canoe out on the dark lake. It felt so good to get out there, I just had to yell. Back at the boat landing, we could see the media lights arrive. The lights allowed us to see more canoes and boats were being put in the water.

We began looking for walleye. Jim was paddling, I was looking for fish. The game wardens saw us and motored over in their powerboat to check us out. They inspected the canoe and didn't see the spear.

I asked if we were under arrest and they said we were not. We said good-bye to them and continued looking for fish. This lake bottom was like the other lake bottoms we had looked at while spearing. It was full of trash. I saw beer cans, a car battery, a padlock, paper or plastic bags, and some other things I couldn't identify. I told my son it used to be a lake when we owned it, now it is just a liquid landfill. We also began to see the reflecting eyes of the walleye. I stood up and began fishing.

The game wardens motored up and said we were under arrest for possessing a spear before May 1. The game wardens were courteous and acted like professional law enforcement officers. We were courteous and acted like professional treaty users. The game wardens confiscated my spear and light.

After our arrest we went back to the landing because it would have been too hard to get fish without a light and spear. We just watched the rest of the arrests. The media were still there gathering news.

When the arrests were over for the evening, we went back to the East Lake Community Center to eat and tell fishing stories. It felt good to see some Shinnobs were willing to stand up for treaty rights.

We got snagged up in the red tape of the state court and began a long series of hearings. Eventually, the state judge threw out the charges against us. I didn't get my spear or light back. I suppose I will have to fill out some forms to get them back, more red tape.

I know a Shinnob who recently had some dealings with a state bureau and their red tape. He compared the experience to a fly learning about flypaper.

It started off easy enough. A neighboring county welfare official called and asked the Shinnob if he could come and speak to his staff about the Anishinaabe. The director of the welfare office offered to pay for his knowledge, mileage, and time. He thought about it and decided he could do it. It was a two-hour gig plus a little trip down the Interstate. Easy money, he thought. Talk for a little while at their workshop then go home and wait for the money. One foot stuck to the flypaper.

He got there early so he could demolish another stereotype about Indians and time. The social workers were just getting ready to sit down for a feast. He was invited to join them and he accepted their invitation. It was a typical white guy feast which means there was no deer or moose meat or beaver. No frybread or wild rice, just a standard grocery store feast. The Shinnob ate good and doubled up at the dessert table. Another foot stuck to the flypaper.

After the meal, a burp, and a smoke, it was time for the Shinnob to sing for his supper. For two hours, the Shinnob told Rez stories. He took the social workers hunting, ricing, and berry picking. He told them drunk and jail stories. The social workers listened with great interest. The Shinnobs in his story were no longer just clients or a caseload, they were humans with a history and some great stories.

When the Shinnob was finished, he was asked to sign a form so he could get his check. He signed and two more feet stuck to the flypaper.

The Shinnob went home and waited for his check. Every day when the mailman drove by, the Shinnob checked his mailbox for the check. After twenty-six trips out to the mailbox, he began to suspect something was wrong. He thought he might have to sign up for welfare until the check came.

The Shinnob called the welfare office and was able to use their toll-free phone number. One foot came loose from the flypaper. The welfare people said they were sorry but, according to their records, the check was already mailed out. The Shinnob said he was sorry too but he didn't get the check. He offered to drive back down to pick up the check. The welfare people told him he would have to wait seven working days. He thought, seven days? According to the white man's Bible, the world was created in just six days. Why the wait?

He waited and after seven working days, he called the welfare office again. That is when he learned that his case had now been turned over to the Fraud Squad investigator. In three working days, the Shinnob got a letter from the welfare office. He was happy until he found out it wasn't a check, it was a summons to appear in their office and swear under oath that he didn't get a check. One wing stuck to the flypaper.

The Shinnob jumped the chain of command and called the director of the welfare office. A meeting was arranged and the Shinnob showed up on time.

The director apologized for the mix-up. He was feeling so bad about the incident, he gave the Shinnob a tour of the welfare office. The director freed the Shinnob from the flypaper and gave him a new check. Of course, this was after the Shinnob signed a notarized form that said he didn't get the original check.

The Shinnob buzzed across the street to the bank and turned the check into green frogskins. While driving home, the Shinnob thought about the month-long ex-

perience and wondered why it is called red tape? It
should be called white tape.

And if dealing with a white bureaucracy isn't scary
enough, we have our own tape to worry about.

The Reservation Business Committee keeps making
rules for their tribal court. They are acting like it was a
real court just like the white man has. We know the difference. The tribal court is bought and paid for by the
RBC.

The RBC passed an official resolution making con-
tempt of court a jail offense. Those found guilty of this
new crime will spend ten days in jail at Nett Lake, the
Reservation north of Fond du Lac.

I wondered why we are so willing to lock up our own
people? Isn't the white man doing a good enough job of
locking up Indians? We are locked up in greater numbers than any other population group in the state. Instead of looking at that problem, the RBC comes up
with a new way to incarcerate us.

Did the state of Minnesota pat the RBC on the head
and call them good little boys because they found a new
way to lock us up? I wonder what the Reservation attorney, Dennis Peterson, would do if hit with a writ from
federal court about locking up Shinnobs.

We are watching to see who goes to jail first for this
new crime. What's next? Jail time for those charged with
aggravated buffoonery with intent to mope?

The treaty rights struggle goes on. This time the
Reservation Business Committee is paying for the
lawyers. The 1837 Treaty is now the subject of federal
court rulings. A judge said the treaty rights exist but an

appeals courts says to wait. We are hoping our leaders are remembering the last treaty struggle.

The abuse of power continues. Chip Wadena, Jerry Rawley, and Rick Clark are now in federal prison. The former members of White Earth's tribal government were found guilty of bid rigging and stealing votes. Three members of the Leech Lake tribal government were involved in an insurance scam. Myron Ellis, Tig Pemberton, and Dan Brown all went to federal prison for their part in the scam. Minnesota Senator Harold "Skip" Finn, the first Anishinaabe to enter the state senate, went to prison for his part in the crime.

We need constitutional reform so we can correct the flaws that let abuses happen. Our form of government is not the best system for managing our affairs but until the RBC decides differently, we are stuck with it. In the last tribal election, I liked all the candidates so much I voted for all of them.

Some of my friends refer to it as the 1934 Indian Reorganization Act Colonial Government. I sometimes agree with them and then remember, "The more corrupt the state, the more numerous the laws." (Tacitus, *Annals*, bk. 111,27.)

8

Warriors

INGIW
MEWINZHA GAA
NANDOBANEJIG

FOR ME, IT started with John Wayne as Sergeant Stryker in *Sands of Iwo Jima.* I wanted to be a marine after seeing that movie. I knew from the old stories that the Anishinaabe were warriors and my family expected me to join the service. As long as I was going to be a warrior, I wanted to be the best.

The marine gunnery sergeant who came to my high school when I was a senior convinced me that I had made the right choice. He was there to recruit for the United States Marine Corps and he warned us that he wanted only the best. I looked at his uniform, it looked so sharp compared to the army, navy, and air force representatives'. The razor creases on the uniform, the polished brass, and shoes so shiny they looked like patent leather, all convinced me I wanted to wear a uniform like that.

After talking with my parents about my plans to be a marine, I got their approval and promised I would go to college when I finished my time in the service. When I graduated from high school, I learned that I was eligible for college scholarships because I was one of the few Indians in the state with a high school diploma. But I wanted to see more of the world before I returned to the classroom.

I signed the enlistment contract while I was still in school under the delayed entry program. I had the summer off and shortly after ricing, I flew to San Diego. It was my first time in an airplane. I didn't even know anyone who had actually flown before.

With my military career off to such a start, I knew I would like it. I learned differently as soon as I got to the Marine Corps Recruit Depot.

Boot camp was physical and mental torture and I hated every minute of the twelve-week process of turning me from a civilian into a marine. The five-mile runs every morning and the five-minute meals all convinced me I had made a mistake when I thought I could be a marine.

Gradually I learned how to get along in my new career. I blended in to survive. I was no longer an Anishinaabe from Minnesota , I was merely another Private in the green machine. It didn't take very long to began thinking like a member of a team.

I remember the endless hours of marching and physical training. I struggled to stay awake in the classrooms where I learned Marine Corps history, military customs, first aid, and weapons. I laughed at myself because I had joined the military to avoid classrooms.

We ran the obstacle course frequently, both as a reward and as punishment. We learned enough in the hand-to-hand combat class, as our instructor said, to get beat up in any bar in the United States. The pugil stick and bayonet course were reminders that I might have to use these skills in a real war. We were convinced the grass grew green because of the blood of marines.

The M-1 rifle was my constant companion. I always knew where my rifle was and how to keep it clean. The rifle was on my shoulder for hours as we learned to move together. When not marching with it, we used it for exercises. It felt like we had done thousands of repetitions of the one called "up and on shoulders."

We had three Drill Instructors who wore Smokey the Bear hats. I will never forget the names of Gunnery Sergeant Wentworth and Sergeants English and Turbeville.

One day Sgt. English marched us to the shot hut where we were inoculated against diseases. It was a small Quonset hut and only a few of us could go in at a time to get our shots. While some were inside, the rest were standing in formation outside. We saw another platoon marching toward us. We could tell they were new in the Marine Corps because they were wearing yellow sweatshirts, green utility pants, white tennis shoes, and green hats pulled down low on their heads. We were salty because we had began to dress like real marines some weeks before.

We watched these new guys. Their Drill Instructor was not happy with their marching because instead of the normal command of "Platoon, Halt!" I heard him say, "Hippity Hop, Mob Stop."

The new recruits were bumping into one another trying to follow the commands. We laughed inside because we knew we'd looked like that just a few weeks before. We couldn't laugh on the outside because if any Drill Instructor saw us, we would have to do many, many push-ups.

When he was done berating the new recruits, the DI leaned his head back so he could see under the brim of his Smokey the Bear hat. He looked at them for a long time before I heard him say in a parade ground voice, "Give me my two singers out here."

Two recruits left the formation and stood in front of the DI and said in unison, "Sir, Private Everly reporting as ordered."

The DI looked at them for a while then said, "Okay Don and Phil, sing me a song."

What? The Everly Brothers were in boot camp? These were the guys I heard singing on the radio all summer before I came to San Diego.

The Everly Brothers started to sing in unison, "Wake up, little Susie, wake up."

Before they got any further into the song, the DI held up his hand to stop them.

"No, no, sing it from the push-up position.

The two new recruits immediately dropped down to the ground and began doing push-ups. While doing the exercise, they started singing again, "Wake up, little Susie, wake up," until they completed the whole song.

When they were done, the DI said, "Thank you very much, now get back into formation and see if you can learn to march as well as you sing."

It took a lot of effort to keep a straight face after watching two highly paid entertainers singing while exercising. Sgt. English came out of the shot hut and caught some of the platoon members smiling. He immediately told us all to drop down and give him forty push-ups. I learned that it is easy to do push-ups if you don't have to sing at the same time.

Boot camp was sometimes violent. I found that out one day when I was detached from the platoon to act as a battalion runner. My job that day was to run messages from the battalion to the various recruit companies. When I was released from my duties I went back to the platoon area. There was no one around. This was scary because it was the first time I had been alone since I got to boot camp. I was confused about what to do next until I saw my platoon lined up in front of the chow hall for supper. I joined them and went inside to eat. While eating, I saw Sgt. English walking over to our table. He looked meanly at us for a minute then said, "Private Northrup, report to the duty hut after chow."

We were at the rifle range and were living in tents while we learned how to shoot the Marine Corps way. After chow, I nervously marched up to the duty hut and in the prescribed manner, knocked on the wooden frame of the tent, and said, "Sir, Private Northrup requests permission to enter the duty hut."

I heard the DI inside growl, "Get your miserable ass in here."

I marched smartly to his desk where he was glaring at me. I didn't know what I had done wrong but I knew I would find out very soon. I stared at the space above his head and said, "Sir, Private Northrup reporting as ordered."

The Drill Instructor didn't say anything for the longest time then got up and walked around the desk to where I was standing at attention. My eyes were looking straight ahead, my shoulders were back, thumbs alongside the seams of my trousers, my feet were at a forty-five degree angle. I was doing everything I was taught in an effort to minimize the punishment I was going to get for some unknown mistake on my part. The DI got very close to my right ear and said loudly, "The Private didn't report in after his duties as a runner."

I started to explain that I was worried about missing chow but before I got the whole sentence out, the DI punched me in the stomach. I wasn't expecting it and went staggering back from the force of the blow. I lurched into the wall of the tent and fell against it. I hit the tent so hard, I actually split the seam in the canvas with my body. I tried grabbing something to keep from falling out of the tent but there was nothing there. I fell through the canvas to the hard ground outside. While trying to catch my breath, I looked up and saw the DI stick his head out of the hole I had made.

"Who the fuck told you to leave the duty hut? Get back in here."

Ignoring the pain in my stomach, I started to climb back through the hole. The DI stopped me and told me to use the door.

I went around to the front, pounded on the door frame, and said loudly, "Sir, Private Northrup requests permission to enter the duty hut."

I heard the DI growl again, "Get in here and this time try to stay until I am done with you."

I marched smartly up to the desk, assumed the position of attention, and said, "Sir, Private Northrup reporting as ordered."

The DI walked over to my right ear and asked if I had anything to say.

"Sir, Private Northrup is reporting back in from being the battalion runner."

It was quiet in the tent for a while until the DI said, "Okay, the next time you will remember to report in, won't you? You bucket of puke."

"Aye, aye sir," I said, clenching my stomach for the next sucker punch. He didn't hit me though. He just yelled in my left ear, "All right, get the fuck out of here.

The cost of a new tent will be taken out of your pay-check, you shit sandwich."

Of course, none of this happened because DI's are not allowed to touch the recruits. Maybe that's why I didn't have to pay for the tent.

Eventually my platoon graduated from boot camp. I was proud as we marched around the grinder, as we learned to call the drill field.

"The Marine's Hymn" rang in my ears and heart as the Recruit Depot Band played the song that all marines know. I had made it through boot camp. I could now call myself a marine.

We were assigned to our next duty station which was Camp Pendleton, just up the coast from San Diego. We learned basic infantry tactics and further skills with the weapons of war we carried. We were in ITR, the Infantry Training Regiment, for a month. Every marine went through it on his way to his permanent duty station. We took a break from training one day to go to a concert.

It was the Everly Brothers who showed up to entertain us. Don or Phil, I don't remember which one, explained they had become marines and had joined a reserve outfit near their homes. They were wearing dress blues. Among the songs they sang was "Wake Up, Little Susie."

I remembered the last time I had heard that song. They looked a lot better this time because they had made it through boot camp too. I recalled the last time I saw someone on stage wearing dress blues. It was that recruiter I met a lifetime ago, way, way back in high school. I wanted to go home, walk up to him, and shake his hand. Then while holding on, I wanted to give him a left cross to the jaw because among other things, I had learned the effectiveness of a sucker punch. He could have told me what to expect in boot camp.

After the Infantry Training Regiment, I was transferred to my permanent duty station, the First Marine Division.

We practiced war in the mountains of southern California for almost a year. I was used to the life of an infantryman. I was lean, mean, and could run all day. I endured the innumerable inspections: rifle inspection, barracks inspection, and the dreaded junk-on-the-bunk, things-on-the-springs inspection. We put everything we were issued out on the bunks. It had to be folded a certain way and laid out in a certain manner. We used pictures from the *Guidebook for Marines* we were issued in boot camp.

I carried the BAR, the Browning automatic rifle. The old salts called it twenty pounds of rust and malfunction. As a bonus, I got to carry a lot more ammunition than the standard infantryman. I was the automatic rifleman for the first fire team of the first squad of the First Platoon of Alpha Company, First Battalion, First Marine Regiment, First Marine Division.

Life was different in southern California than it was in Minnesota when I had lived on the Fond du Lac Reservation. It seemed like a long time ago but was actually only about six months or so. I very quickly found out who the other Indians were in my area.

There was a Navajo from New Mexico named Ted Charles in my company. We found a Comanche from Oklahoma named Hugh Chebahtah. We hung around with one another because we were the only Indians around. Ted had a sister, Amelia Lewis, who lived in Los Angeles. We spent a lot of our off-duty time at her house. She mothered us, kept us fed, worried about us when we were out, and scolded us when we made mistakes. She felt like family. Once on the way to Amelia's house, Hugh said, "Back home I live in Mean Canyon. The farther up the canyon you go, the meaner we get. Mine is the last house, my bedroom's on the far side."

We were eighteen, nineteen years old as we explored Hollywood, San Diego, Long Beach, and any other place we could go in the time we had off.

The time off ended when President Kennedy came on TV to tell us Castro had missiles in Cuba. Being marines, we knew we would be the first ones into Cuba. In the frenzy of the mount-out, we were issued new M-14 rifles to replace the World War II vintage M-1s and BARs we carried.

We went to San Diego to get on a troop ship. Before we left we had the obligatory speech by a general. He told us our new name was the Fifth Marine Expeditionary Brigade. He also told us the initials stood for Make 'em Break. We left the Port of San Diego and sailed south along the coast of Baja, California.

At first, we were alone. The USS *Henrico*, APA 45, the navy's designation for this attack transport, sailed south. The sailors on board seemed unusually proud of the fact that this was the oldest troop ship still on active duty. They also told us they usually carried and landed eight hundred troops. There were twelve hundred marines on the ship. One morning we saw that a U.S. Navy destroyer had joined us while we slept. The next morning there were three more. Next, it was an aircraft carrier and tankers that became part of our convoy.

We came to the Panama Canal and all the ships lined up to go through. Seeing it up close was interesting for me because just a short while before in high school, I had studied it. I impressed my fellow marines when I told them the names of the locks and lakes we were going through. At one of the locks, we got off the ship and ran alongside in formation. The Americans who lived in the Canal Zone came to see us make the transit. They were waving American flags and cheering us as we went by.

On the *Henrico*, we spent most of our time standing in line. Stand in line for food, for a shower, for the movie. We fired our rifles off the fantail of the ship so we could learn how the new rifles worked. The marines exercised in the cramped spaces as the sailors ran the ship. Sometimes the sailors had drills like "General Quarters." Each sailor had an assigned place to be. It was all worked out beforehand. If a sailor had to go to the fantail, he used one side of the ship to get there. If he had to go to the bow, he used the other side. We watched these drills for a while before we made our move. We'd grab a couple of the sailors running by and just hold them until they were late reporting in to their assigned position.

We stayed offshore Cuba for five days and nights, as I recall. We were preparing to make an amphibious assault to help remove the missiles. There were a lot of preparations made to help us in our assault. We had maps, pictures, a scale model of the beach defenses, and a feeling that we were really going in.

"A" Company's mission was to take the first row of bunkers. The waves of marines landing behind us would take the second row and so on until there were no more bunkers. Like a fool, during one of the briefings I asked what our mission was after taking the first row. The major giving the briefing told me we would no longer be effective as a fighting force. It took a while to sink in that we marines in the first wave would all be dead.

We didn't have to invade Cuba because the missiles were removed. Instead we went to the island of Vieques, a part of Puerto Rico, where we practiced an amphibious landing. By this time we had been aboard ship for over a month. After playing war, our leaders turned us loose for R & R in a town called Isabel Segunda.

After a few days there drinking rum, we went to Kingston, Jamaica. During the day we were serious tourists. The other Indians and I hung out together and toured the Governor's Palace. Outside there was a living maze made from hedges. We got in there and couldn't find our way out. I looked up and found the sun and followed it straight out of the maze. We all got a little scratched up from crashing through the hedges but we got out. After touring all day we drank rum. We didn't stay long enough in Kingston for me, all too soon we got back on the ship.

Thanksgiving came while we were at sea. We had a huge turkey dinner with all the trimmings including dysentery. All twelve hundred Marines who ate that meal got sick. There was one officer who got diarrhea from the meal. It was the Officer of the Day whose duty it was to eat with the troops. The intestinal problems started a couple hours after the meal. I went to the head, as we called the bathroom, because my guts were roiling, gurgling, and cramping. When I got there I was surprised to see lines in front of every toilet. As soon as one marine got up, another rushed to his place and sat down. I was standing in line waiting my turn when the marine in front of me couldn't wait. He reached up and snatched the cover, as marines call a hat, from the guy in front of him and squatted down and filled it. He told the coverless marine, "Okay, I owe you a cover, now hand me some toilet paper."

The Medical Corpsmen were standing there with bottles of a white, chalky liquid. As soon as a marine got up, they gave him a double tablespoonful of the stuff. The smell in the heads was getting pretty rank and some guys got sick from the smell. They had liquid coming out of both ends.

Marines were finding quiet little corners to take care of their business when they didn't have time to stand in line. The only place it didn't smell on the ship was at the extreme front end of the bow.

I went out on the deck to get some air in between my turns at the toilet. Marines were in sleeping bags out on the deck because of the overcrowding on the ship. I saw one guy struggling to get the zipper open on his bag. I saw him relax and quit trying to get the bag open. After a while he calmly opened the bag, stood up, and took his trousers and skivies off. He threw the sleeping bag and clothing over the rail of the ship.

The sailors were really mad at us marines. As I recall, they spent three days with high pressure hoses cleaning up after us.

I was glad when we made the transit back through the Panama Canal. I would have rather faced the machine guns of the Cubans than spend another day on that ship. We off-loaded in California and went back to practicing war in the mountains.

After a while we became a transplacement battalion and traded places with another battalion that was stationed in Okinawa. We spent twenty-one days crossing the Pacific and I remembered why I didn't want to be a sailor.

I knew nothing of Okinawa except what I had heard from old salts who had been stationed there before. It had been the site of one of the last major battles of World War II according to the history books.

The people I met on the island were those who made their living from the U.S. military presence, the cab drivers, bartenders, and the bar girls. They seemed happy to see us there, spending money. At least once a week, an Okinawan would look at me and speak Japanese as if expecting me to understand.

We spent a thirteen-month tour of duty there. We took side trips to Camp Fuji, Japan. I got a chance to climb Mt. Fuji, a sacred mountain of the Japanese. We got to explore Tokyo and the countryside, too.

We also made an amphibious landing at Kaohsiung, Taiwan. When I came off the landing craft, I saw a man who looked like Chiang Kai-shek watching the landing. He resembled the man I had seen in the newsreels and pictures. We practiced war in the hills for a week and then boarded the ship again.

We landed in Subic Bay in the Philippines where we practiced war in the jungles. One part of it was called survival training. We had a Negrito guide who showed us how to make shelters, catch fish, and live off the land. One day our guide taught us how to eat bats. First, we had to find a bamboo tree with holes in it, then chop it down quickly. Then grab the little creatures when they came out, kill them, and roast them on a stick. We were hungry and got over the thought of eating bats. With enough salt, they didn't taste bad. I learned that if one goes without food long enough, there is no telling what one will eat.

We were still practicing war in the Philippines when a gunshot in Dallas, Texas, changed history. The same president that forced Russia and Cuba to back down during the Missile Crisis was now a victim of violence. We mourned Jack Kennedy.

One thing I noticed in my travels was that it didn't matter what country I was in, some person there would come up and speak their language to me. I guess I looked like a native wherever we went. I would explain that I was an Anishinaabeg from northern Minnesota and we would share a laugh about their mistake. We usually would then spend time trying to learn each other's language after comparing skin, hair, and eye color. I learned a smattering of Spanish, Japanese, Chinese, and Tagalog.

After the tour of duty was over I came back to the United States and reported into my next duty station at Barstow, California. I had been a military policeman for a little over a year when the Third Battalion, Ninth Marines landed in Da Nang, South Vietnam.

After practicing war for almost four years, I knew that was the place for me because I wasn't getting any warrior experience in the Mojave Desert. I extended my enlistment so I would have enough time for a tour of duty in South Vietnam.

Once again I crossed the Pacific Ocean. We flew in a windowless, converted air force tanker. There were six rows of seats and we faced the rear of the plane. We made a refueling stop at Wake Island. I remembered that John Wayne had also made a WW II movie about that place. We were allowed to get out and stretch. I noticed that the whole island stands out of the ocean about five feet at the most.

It took us eighteen hours of flying time to get to Da

Nang. Because of the time zones and international date line, we got there fifteen minutes before we left.

The plane landed at Da Nang Air Base and I reported in. I was sent to the Ninth Marine Regimental Headquarters and they sent me to the Third Battalion. I was further transferred to India Company. I was apprehensive but I knew I was well trained after four years of practicing war. I also knew I could depend on my fellow marines.

I was issued an M-14 rifle and my 782 gear, a marine term for cartridge belt, canteens, poncho, and the rest of the field equipment. As soon as I settled in, I began hearing stories of all the marines who had died before I got there. The old salts who had been in country before me seemed happy to fill me in on the details of each marine's death.

At first, we were in a perimeter south of the air base then we were pulled back to guard the airstrip itself. My introduction to the war was the sound of rockets impacting on the air base. We were there for a while, then we were once again transferred to Marble Mountain southeast of Da Nang. While we were there I climbed one of the mountains to look at the Buddhist temples and the famous caves. After that we went to a combat base about four miles south of Marble Mountain.

This was a sprawling base surrounded by a huge sand berm built by the Seabees. We traveled by chopper and truck, but mostly on foot. One night, a squad from our company had a successful ambush when they intercepted some Viet Cong who were on their way to blow up helicopters at Marble Mountain. By this time I was used to seeing wounded and dead people. The first time I was shocked but I stayed cool because I knew the other marines were watching me. After it happened a few times, I was no longer horrified. I would look down at the dead person, Asian or American, and think—Jeez, I'm glad that's you lying there and not me. I was seeing terrible wounds mostly from mines but some gunshots also.

I was a grunt, a rifleman in the United States Marine Corps. One version of why we were called grunts is because of the noise made when putting on your pack, or pulling your leg out of the mud. Mud marines. We sarcastically called ourselves USMC—Uncle Sam's Misguided Children. We didn't know it then but we were the bayonet end of America's foreign policy.

We recognized the look in one another's eyes. The look that said this marine has seen the worst things imaginable. We didn't know we were making lifelong memories. We were marines, young, strong, with a feeling of being bulletproof. It always happened to the other guy, we thought. That feeling went away with each wounded marine we loaded on a helicopter.

I was at times scared, tired, thirsty, sleepy, bored, horrified, hungry. Sometimes, all at the same time. I was more afraid of getting wounded than being killed. Tired because grunts carry heavy things and walk a lot, thirsty because sometimes there was only rice paddy water to drink, bored between the explosions or gunshots, horrified by what was happening around me, and hungry because we only ate C-rations.

There were twelve different meals. Each came with an accessory pouch which contained toilet paper, matches, sugar, salt, a white plastic spoon, and four cigarettes.

I learned to like the one called Ham and Lima Beans.

Most grunts hated even looking at the greasy water on top and would throw it away rather than eat it. I liked Ham and Lima Beans because I was hungry as a child and never wasted food. The best part of C-rations were the peaches, of course. The John Wayne crackers weren't bad when smeared with the cheese spread. We called the little can opener that came with the rations a P-38. I used to wear one on my dog tag chain.

My dog tags identified me, my serial number, my job, and blood type. I taped them together so they wouldn't make noise.

It didn't take me long to develop what we called the turtle reflex. That is the involuntary act of trying to duck your head into your chest cavity. We were at the sand berm combat base when I heard a loud noise. I looked and ducked at the same time.

I saw part of a marine flying through the air. His legs were still standing and then they fell over. The body continued up and then came back down. When he hit the sand, I saw him try to push himself up. The marine was near the back of an Ontos, a tracked vehicle which carries six 106mm recoilless rifles. A blast comes out the back of the weapon also. He had been standing behind one when it went off. The blast blew his body in half and some of us were detailed to help pick up the pieces of what used to be a man. We found large chunks scattered over a wide area and the only way we could find the smaller parts was to see where the flies were landing. Once again it was—Jeez, I'm glad that was you and not me time.

We left that combat base and went to An Hoa on a combat operation called Operation Georgia. We were flying in a Chinook helicopter when I felt something thump under my left foot. I happened to be looking down at the time when I saw a hole appear in the floor between my feet. Quickly realizing what had happened, I looked up at the roof of the chopper to see where it went out. I didn't see any holes anywhere. Then I looked at the cases of grenades stacked in front of me. The bullet had come up at an angle and went into the top case of frags, as we called grenades. I carefully opened the case to check for damage. I found one grenade that had a hole through the outside black cardboard tube. Even more carefully, I took the frag out. The outside sheet metal was pierced, the C-4 explosive was pushed away, and I could see the blasting cap down the center. I carried it over to the window and threw it out of the chopper. After it was gone we looked for the bullet to see what size it was. We found it stuck in the wooden crate that held 3.5-inch Willy Peter rocket rounds. That was one of those times when I was scared for a long time after it was over. If that bullet had touched the blasting cap of the grenade, the explosion would have blown the chopper in half and we would have quit flying all of a sudden. There were ten guys on that chopper and it would have been raining human and helicopter parts all over the rice paddies east of An Hoa.

Our days were spent patrolling and our nights were spent in ambush positions. At night, we slept for two hours and were awake for two hours. I learned to fall asleep fast and wake up even faster. The area we were in was called a free fire zone, which meant the civilians had been removed leaving only the Viet Cong and the North Vietnamese Army.

Once while we were on a patrol, a Vietnamese man got up from behind a rice paddy dike and began to run from us. He was about fifty feet away when he started running. The man looked military age. He wasn't carrying a weapon but was considered an enemy because he was running.

We began shouting and shooting at him as he ducked, dodged, zigged, and zagged across the paddy. The bullets were hitting all around him as he continued to run. Our machine gunner was firing three-round bursts from the hip. The red tracer rounds were streaking out of the M-60. The assistant gunner carrying the 3.5 rocket launcher came up and fired at him. He had a white phosphorus round loaded and when he fired, he pulled the rocket launcher down. The rocket round hit the ground right in front of us and exploded. We had to duck to escape the pieces of burning phosphorus from the explosion. The Vietnamese man was able to get farther away from us because now he was hidden by a cloud of white smoke from the explosion. The rocket team leader grabbed the weapon and fired a HEAT (high explosive antitank) round at the man who was now about five hundred meters away. We saw the rocket arc up and come back down next to the running man's feet. It didn't explode and just splashed paddy water on him. The rocket round went bouncing across the rice paddy, a dud. We had to quit shooting at him because someone else began shooting at us from behind. Later on, we talked about it and decided we wanted to be there when the man told his grandchildren about the time he met some marines during the war.

One night at An Hoa, while sitting on the perimeter, we heard our artillery firing just to the west of the combat base. The shelling seemed to go on a long time and we were glad when it was over because we didn't know

what was going on. In the morning we found out. Someone thought they heard enemy troops moving around so
they called in artillery on the noise. Our job the next
morning was to go out and count and stack up the bodies that were killed. We went out and around the little
lake. The jungle got progressively thicker and before
long we were wading along the shore of the lake. A ra-
dioman stepped in a hole in the lake and disappeared.
The only thing the marines could see was the antenna
from his radio. They used it to haul him out of the hole.

While we were wading along the shore, the water got
deeper and deeper. The artillery had killed quite a few
fish in the lake and they were floating on the surface. I
remembered blowing the dead fish away from my
mouth; I couldn't use my hands because I was carrying
my rifle. The guy who was walking point suddenly let
loose with a twenty-round burst. It is hard to dive for
cover when walking in water up to your chin. We made
it to shore and tried to blend into the brush. After a
while the word came down, the point man had fired at
a snake, a very large one. When I came by where the
snake was lying, I looked and estimated the size of the
snake. He was as big around as my thigh. We didn't
stick around long enough to determine if the artillery
had killed him or if it had been the point man shooting.
I had dreams of that snake for many nights after. We
never did find any bodies to count or stack up. The
nights and the days dragged on and on.

One morning at An Hoa our squad was detailed to
take a little walk. It was just a short walk around the
perimeter to gather the Claymore directional mines. We
set the mines out at night to help seal gaps in the
perimeter. Sometimes the Viet Cong would crawl up

and turn the mines around so they were facing the marines. Just before we set out to go beyond the wire, the platoon commander told us to wait. Here is what happened:

The Duke

"Hold up on that patrol,
we got a chopper coming in."
Good, no reason to stand
so we all sat down.
The slapping sound of the rotor
blades told us a landing was near.
Two gunships went over
looking for danger to the
chopper they were escorting.
It landed, they walked in our direction.
Starched jungle utilities, spit-shined boots,
shiny rank insignia
told us these were rear echelon marines.
They surrounded a large green clad man.
"It's John Fucking Wayne," one grunt said.
The Duke centered himself in
the circle of men, smiling, posing for pictures and
signing autographs.
He was enjoying himself until
the Indian patrol leader
invited him for a walk with the grunts.
The Duke patted his ample belly and said,
"Heh, heh, heh, I'll leave that to you
professionals."
John Fucking Wayne, who killed
Indians by the dozens
with his movie sixshooter, refused.

The ranking officers looked
at the disrespectful marines.
Court martials and other
punishments filtered through
their rear echelon brains.
The grunts looked back with,
wha cha gonna do? Cut my
hair and send me to Vietnam?
I'm already here, maybe for the rest of my life.
The Duke looked troubled
when he saw the killing
etched in the eyes of the young grunts,
more killing than he had seen
in a quarter century of movie killing.
The Duke gave some excuse about lung cancer
and was excused from the rest of the war.
Derisive laughter lifted the chopper away
from the young grunts.
"What a pussy, wouldn't even
go on a little walk with us."

I was disappointed that the Duke wouldn't take a little walk with me and the mud marines. I wanted to be able to tell my family that I had been on a patrol with John Wayne.

The nights were the scariest. We would walk all day and set up our night defensive positions just before dark. We would use our entrenching tools to scrape out fighting positions. As soon as it got dark, we would move to another hill and once again dig in. While sitting there, we would sometimes look back and hear enemy mortars and machine guns hitting the hill we left. We knew we were always under enemy observation.

One night we got the word to get up and start walking. We were going to be the anvil for a force of marines that were sweeping through. They were the hammer and we were hoping to crush the enemy troops between us. It was about 3:00 A.M. when we started walking to get in position. We walked all day until about two o'clock in the afternoon (1400 hours as they say in the military). We set up a perimeter and the choppers came to resupply us. The ammo came out first, then the drinking water. Finally we saw a large chopper approaching with a pallet of C-rations. We were already loaded down with as much as we could carry. We didn't know what to do with all that food. The marines went through the pallet and removed all the food we liked, but there was still a lot left. We didn't want to leave it for the enemy so someone suggested we blow it up. The demolition people stacked many pounds of C-4 (plastic explosive) around the food and once we were far enough away, they set it off. The resulting explosion did nothing but scatter the little green cans all over the rice paddy. We walked all day until 11:00 that night. We didn't find any enemy troops that day either. The common sentiment was we would chase the Viet Cong or NVA until they caught us.

For us, being in a combat zone was either boring or exciting. When things were happening, it was very, very exciting. When things were quiet and we weren't moving, we would sometimes play with fragmentation grenades. We'd experiment with the grenades, holding them for a while before throwing them, trying for an airburst. If a new marine joined us we would indoctrinate him into the war with a frag. There is a way to put a piece of wire in the firing mechanism of a grenade to keep it from going off. Once fixed like that, the spoon would fly off the grenade but it wouldn't explode because of the wire. Then someone would go up to the new marine and tell him he was having trouble getting the pin back in the grenade and ask for help. As he handed it to the new marine, he would drop it on the ground. I never saw one dive on a grenade to protect his buddies. It was nothing but assholes and elbows as marines dove away from the anticipated blast. It was always good for a laugh.

When getting hit by enemy mortars, there is really nothing to do but hide from the explosions and count them going off. On the night of my birthday we got hit with twenty-three rounds, the same number as my years. I wondered how the bad guys knew it was my birthday.

Sometimes while sitting in a hole on a perimeter, we would hear someone outside our positions pounding on a piece of wood. In the dark, a noise like that would make everyone tense. The adrenaline would flow when we heard the unusual noise. Then we would hear someone else on the other side of the perimeter answer the first one by pounding on a piece of wood. At times, they were all around the positions we occupied. We never knew if it was one or two people or the beginning of a major attack. Sometimes we would see a light while trying to stare through the darkness. We couldn't shoot because we didn't want to give our position away. We thought the Viet Cong or the North Vietnamese Army was putting the lights there to unnerve us. It worked.

It didn't take very long to learn what bullets sound like when they go by. I was already familiar with the sound because we used to pull targets at the rifle range when we were practicing for war. Pulling targets means to lower the targets, patch the holes, and raise them back up again. When bullets are far away they make a buzzing noise when they go by. When they go by closely they make a cracking noise followed by the sound of the weapon that fired it.

Bullets and explosives were not the only danger in that combat area. We had to worry about punji sticks: needle-sharp pieces of wood, usually a foot to two feet long, stuck into the ground. The sharp end is flame-hardened. They also had human or water buffalo feces smeared on them to cause a septic infection. They were usually placed on the side of the trail where marines dove for cover whenever the shooting started. I never came close to getting punctured by one but I did see one unfortunate South Vietnamese soldier who fell into a pit that contained punji sticks. This guy didn't have to worry about septic infection because the stick entered his groin and came out his neck. The sides of the pit were clawed up where he tried to pull himself off the primitive weapon. He bled to death before we could get him off. I knew exactly when he died because his bowels let go as we were trying to lift him off the stick.

In addition to the man-made hazards, there was the weather. During the monsoon season it would rain all day and then all night. The only time it didn't was a half hour or so in the morning and then a half hour in the afternoon. The rest of the time it rained. During the dry part of the year, it was hot. We didn't have a thermometer but I knew the temperature was over one hundred degrees. When it was hot, I wished for the rain; when it was raining, I wished for the hot.

After being in country for quite a few months, my turn to go on R & R came up. Since I had been to Japan before, I chose to go there again.

I went back to Da Nang, dug around in the seabag and found some khakis to wear until I got to Japan. I waited until my flight was called and climbed up the steps to the civilian airplane that was to take me away from the craziness of war.

I found a seat next to a marine who was wearing a Silver Star on his chest. I sat next to this genuine hero and noted that he had a Purple Heart with a star in the middle. Not only was this marine a hero, but he was a wounded hero besides.

After a while we started to talk while waiting for the plane to take off. I asked him what outfit he was with. He said, "Third Battalion, Ninth Marines."

I said I was from that outfit too. I asked him what company he was in since I had never seen him before. He replied, "India Company, I'm the first squadleader of the First Platoon."

I was surprised because he named my job title. I told him that I was the first squadleader of the First Platoon also. Then I asked him where he was really from.

"Actually, I'm in the Third Marine Air Wing. I work on airplanes."

I told him if he had picked any other company in the battalion I wouldn't have known he was bullshitting. I asked him how he had earned the Silver Star. He said, "I got these at the PX because I thought they would look good on my uniform."

I suggested that he take them off before the real grunts, the infantrymen, heard that he was not who he appeared to be. He took the medals off and left to sit in another part of the airplane. I didn't see him anymore after that.

I thoroughly enjoyed Tokyo, Japan. I had fifteen hundred dollars and five days to spend it. The last time I was in Japan, I heard about Kobe beef. The cows are massaged every day and are fed beer. I wanted to taste this because I hadn't the last time. After eating out of little green C-ration cans for eight months, I wanted real food.

I found a restaurant that offered Kobe beef. I ordered the biggest steak they had. I began eating and it didn't take too long to finish the meal. Since I had been going without real food for so long, I decided to have another. When I ordered the second one, the waiters told the cook who came out of the kitchen to watch this Indian marine eat. The beef was everything I expected it to be.

My time in Japan was haunted by the fact that I had to go back to the war in just a few days. Determined to make the most of the time I had left, I went to Tokyo Tower to look at the smog.

On the way to the tower, I was walking by a department store, looking in the window and admiring myself because I looked so clean. No helmet, no rifle, no canteens or ammo pouches. Just a young jarhead wearing civilian clothes bopping down the crowded street. I didn't see the kids behind me with the firecrackers. When I heard the noise, I did a dive and roll and came up facing the noise. From my prone position on the sidewalk, I could see my reflection in the store window as I was frantically reaching for my rifle.

I was embarrassed because the polite Japanese opened up and cleared a space and I was lying in a circle of curious pedestrians. I regained my feet, hailed a cab, and quickly left the scene.

On top of the Tokyo Tower, there are thick glass panels in the floor. I stepped out on one and could see all the way to the ground straight under my feet. I did an emergency dive and roll and came up clutching both sides of the window frame. My feet and eyes were having an argument. My feet said it was safe but my eyes said different. Once again, the polite Japanese opened up and formed a circle around me as I was lying there, holding on.

I don't remember too much more of Tokyo because I was in an alcohol haze. I remembered to buy great quantities of white socks. I knew the troops back in the rice paddy mud would appreciate new, clean, white socks.

The war returned as soon as I got back to Da Nang Air Base. My plane circled the runway while fighter jets took off to bomb North Vietnam.

I reported back to my company and immediately updated my short-timer's calendar. Before too long I realized I was a double-digit midget. This meant I had less than one hundred days left in Vietnam. I was now even more careful because I wanted to go home. I took no chances. If I heard a noise that didn't sound right, I threw a grenade. That was my solution to the problem of noises outside the perimeter at night. One morning I counted three pigs, probably Viet Cong pigs, I had killed with my grenades.

I eventually left Vietnam. Unlike so many I had seen, I still had all my body parts. I left Vietnam with the right number of legs and arms. The part I didn't like was leaving all my friends from India Company, my foxhole buddies. We all said we would get together some time and stay in touch but we didn't.

When I got back to the world, as we called the United States, I learned not to bring up the subject of Vietnam anywhere, anytime. I kept quiet about my experiences in the war. No one wanted to hear and I didn't want to tell.

About a year after the war I was watching television and saw John Wayne in *Sands of Iwo Jima.* After the movie ended, I got ready for inspection. I dug out my dress blues uniform and prepared. First, I washed the white parts, the belt, the cover, and gloves. I dug out my last can of Brasso and made my brass shine, as my DI used to say, like a diamond in a goat's ass. My shoes looked like mirrors after hours of spit-shining. I hung my shooting badges and medals on the blouse in the prescribed manner and got dressed after ironing the creases.

I looked in the mirror for a while then went outside and crawled under my Austin Healy sports car and changed the oil.

Veterans

OGICHIDAG

I WAS IN full blown denial about Vietnam for at least fifteen years. I had Post Traumatic Stress Disorder before it had a name. I traveled to escape the stink of war before returning home.

I came back to the Rez in the late '70s and like a lot of Vietnam veterans, went to the woods. On and off for six years, I lived in a tipi, a mile from the nearest blacktop. The tipi was set up on the shore of Perch Lake, a suburb of Sawyer. It was where my grandfather, Joe Northrup, lived when he was a young man. My dad grew up there. I was home. The loons sang and welcomed me back.

First, I had to learn how to put up the tipi. We're wigwam people. I knew how to build those but the tipi was a challenge. My brothers, cousins, and friends helped. It took us all of one day to figure out how to properly set it up. We were done hanging the door when the sun was going down across the lake.

We built a fire inside the tipi. From the outside it

looked like a huge lampshade, glowing from the light of the fire. The smell of wood smoke told me I was where I was supposed to be.

Living in the tipi away from the noises of civilization was what I needed after all my wanderings. The quiet was alive with the sound of the water gurgling on the shoreline, the wind in the trees, and the animal noises.

I could hear visitors coming down the road that came to be called Oil Pan Alley. The rough road kept the riff-raff out and only friends and relatives made the trek to the tipi. We'd entertain ourselves by telling stories. All kinds of stories. Hunting, fishing, fighting stories. We'd listen to old stories of the Anishinaabeg. We were inventing new stories to tell around the fire at the tipi.

One evening I was making some notes about the story I was going to tell the next time I had company. When I looked at my notes, I realized it wasn't too much different from the stories in a book. I thought I could make a story out of my notes so I sat up all night writing and rewriting. The next time I had relatives visiting, I read the story to them. They were falling off the log laughing so I knew I was onto something. I wrote some more until I had fourteen stories. Gerald Vizenor, Anishinaabeg author, was editing a book called *Touchwood* and wanted to see my stories. I sent him what I had and he put them in the book. Then I was a published writer and had to learn more about what I was doing.

Thinking that I was too old to be working construction, I thought I'd see if I could make my living by writing. The Reservation hired me as their newspaper editor. It was a one-man show. I wrote the stories, took the pictures, updated the mailing list, laid out the two-page issue, made the coffee, and talked a lot on the phone.

I courted and married a Dakota woman named Patricia Dow. A family joke goes that I paid the bride price in horses. I gave my mother-in-law a three-and-a-half-horsepower lawn mower. My new bride said, "I'm not living in a tipi, I want a house."

We live in a frame house on Northrup Road in the village of Sawyer among family. It has been said that you can't throw a rock without hitting a cousin of some sort. We like the quiet of small town living and I can't even imagine living anywhere else.

In 1986, I began calling myself a freelance writer. For the longest time, I struggled to make a living, but eventually I began to get money for my words. When my first book, *Walking the Rez Road*, won a Minnesota Book Award, and a Northeast Minnesota Book Award, I knew I had made the right choice.

The Fond du Lac Follies, my contribution to journalism, has been running since 1986. The syndicated column gives me a chance to share my views on life with readers who are interested in the lives of the Anishinaabeg.

After living back home on the Reservation for a few years, I began to realize that being a veteran was not something to be ashamed of. The honor songs at every powwow made me remember how Anishinaabe people feel about their veterans.

In the mid-80s, I went to the big Welcome Home parade for Vietnam vets in Chicago. Once I got there, I had a difficult choice to make. Do I march with the veterans from the Third Marine Division or with the American Indians? Naturally, I chose to walk with the Indians.

It felt like we were finally being welcomed home by

America. The people applauding us made me feel like I had done something right when I went to war. I began to think of forgiving America for Vietnam.

After Chicago, I got more involved in veterans' doings. In 1990, my wife and I motored to Lame Deer, Montana. We went there to attend the Ninth Annual Vietnam Era Veteran Inter-Tribal Association powwow. The name of the group was almost as long as the war. The event was hosted by the Morning Star Chapter led by Windy Shoulderblade.

We drove from Minnesota to Montana in our big, blue '67 Buick. How ironic, I thought. This car was being built while I was in the war. It was originally a Rez car that survived to become a classic, almost a collector's item.

The planning for the trip took about two minutes once I told my wife I wanted to go to a veteran's powwow. She agreed, then wanted to know where and how far? I told her Montana and according to the map, about 860 miles. We left right away.

The directions were simple enough. Get on Interstate 94 and hang a left just past Forsyth, Montana.

To do that we had to leave the woods of Minnesota and drive across North Dakota. Along the way we passed the North Dakota State Forest and saw both trees. In Jamestown, we saw the world's largest buffalo. Somewhere along the Interstate, we saw a sign advertising the world's largest Holstein cow. We wondered who had to clean up after these huge critters?

There were the usual summertime construction zones with the orange-clad workers. We saw an airplane spraying crops. Other than that, there wasn't much to see in North Dakota.

After the left just past Forsyth, we drove south to the powwow grounds in Lame Deer. Everyone was still sleeping so we decided on a side trip to Little Bighorn Battlefield National Monument. It was a short forty-mile ride through the Rosebud Mountains.

The cost for getting Five Deer through the gates was three bucks. I thought it would be cheap at twice the price.

We parked next to a Chimook driving a Winnebago camper. He was pulling a Dakota truck behind the R.V. The site of the best known battle of the Lakota and Cheyenne was visited by a Winnebago with a Dakota. This Anishinaabe also brought a Dakota—my wife, not a truck.

After we toured the museum, we basked in reflected glory. We took pictures and honored the Lakota and Cheyenne warriors who fought here. At one point, I got swept up in the emotion and wanted to yell, "Way to go, Indians!"

Yelling would have disturbed the somber-looking white tourists. The R.V. drivers and passengers were walking around like they were in church or at a funeral. Most had their faces set in a half frown. They talked quietly among themselves. I was walking along just proud.

We enjoyed the battlefield tour. As an infantryman, I studied the terrain. The battle looked like a classic double envelopment. Chief Gall led one side and Chief Crazy Horse led the other. The U.S. Army Cavalry troops were buried where they fell. The white stone markers were scattered in the brown rolling hills.

"Look, two more got it over there," said a Shinnob.

While touring the battlefield, I remembered every bad

Custer joke I had ever heard. In one, he was well dressed for the occasion, wearing an Arrow shirt; or he was half right when he boasted about riding through the Indian nation, he only made it halfway through Lakota country.

On our way out of the monument, we stopped at the museum to have another look at the memorial erected by Indian activists. It honored the warriors who fought there.

We left the dead at the battlefield and joined the living in Lame Deer. Along the way we stopped to pick sage. We got back to town just in time for the parade.

The Cheyenne people lined both sides of the street in a drizzling rain. A little water didn't stop them from honoring their veterans. Camouflage jackets and ribbon shirts marched together in the parade. Veterans carried American and tribal flags, POW/MIA flags, and even a couple of Marine Corps flags. Somehow our big, blue Buick brought up the rear of the parade. My wife Pat drove along waving to the crowd.

After the rain ended, the dancing began at the Kenneth Beartusk Memorial powwow grounds.

It was a good celebration. There were honoring songs and giveaways all afternoon. It was almost thirteen straight hours of honoring veterans. The eating, dancing, and singing continued long past dark in the mountains of the Cheyenne.

We felt good and bad as we left the powwow. Good, because of the way we were honored as veterans. Bad, because we had to drive through North Dakota to get home. Good, because we were riding in the big, blue Buick named Five Deer. Bad, because we didn't know how long the car would last.

Through the moccasin telegraph, I heard that some Russian veterans of the Afghan War were traveling through northern Minnesota with Vietnam vets. I found out they would be at the Grand Portage Reservation so I joined them. Gary Kent, known locally as Fuzzy, came along. He was a jarhead who had been in Khe Sanh, among other places. We pulled into the parking lot of the Grand Portage Lodge and saw the Russian flag flying up there with the flags from Canada and the United States. After forty years of the Cold War, we were curious about meeting Russians.

We got there just in time for the banquet. Everyone else was on the dessert course, but after some fancy knife and fork work we caught up.

The veterans went to the powwow where we were honored by dancers and spectators. The Russians danced one round then split up to watch the doings. Using interpreters and a lot of body language, we told war stories. It turned out these veterans weren't really Russians, they were from Latvia. They seemed very interested in the Anishinaabe they saw at Grand Portage. They asked about the dancing, the dance outfits, and the language. They'd read about us but had never met any of us. We traded frybread for postcards and dollars for rubles. The Latvians said they would tell their relatives about the Anishinaabe they met at Grand Portage.

We had one thing in common—the turtle reflex. All the veterans learned that bullets and shrapnel are the same regardless of the ideological cause or location.

Just for grins I taught the guys from Latvia what I called the minefield dance. I put a finger in each ear, closed my eyes, and patted the ground in front of me

with my left foot. When they were walking to their van
to leave, two of them stopped and did a real good Lat-
vian version of the minefield dance.

As a veteran I was very interested when the Iraqi
forces invaded Kuwait. I watched closely as the American war machine began to gear up. I was especially worried because my son, Matthew, was then a grunt. He
was stationed in Alaska and he called to let us know he
would be getting on an airplane for the desert. It made
perfect military sense to me, take troops that are training in snow and send them to the sand.

He called later that day and said he didn't have to go
to war in the gulf. A couple of hours later he called again
to say he was going.

The phone calls went on for a week. One time he was
going and the next he wasn't. As I recall, he was calling
collect too. He didn't have to go and we were relieved
when it was over.

I wrote a poem called,

Gulf Oil

The start of the war was big news last month
It was on all the TV stations for three whole
days
They didn't even break for commercials
After three days, the regular programming
came back on
It started with the soap operas
I wondered about that when
the titles of the soaps jumped out at me
ALL MY CHILDREN have but ONE
LIFE TO LIVE,

We know they need a strong
GUIDING LIGHT in these
DAYS OF OUR LIVES but
AS THE WORLD TURNS,
We don't want them to end up in a
GENERAL HOSPITAL in
SANTA BARBARA or anywhere else
We know they are the
YOUNG AND RESTLESS and
BOLD AND BEAUTIFUL but
we pray they come home safe and soon.

At first I tried to ignore the Gulf War but that proved impossible. I wrote some rambling, disconnected war thoughts from my point of view as an Anishinaabeg, a veteran, and a father.

Honor the warriors but not the war makers. A very difficult concept. We sent our best and brightest to the gulf. Once the ground war started, I wondered how many would come back undamaged in body or mind? Only time will tell if the sacrifices will be worth it.

I felt like we were stroked into the war by the media, especially television. My TV told me we went there to defend Saudi Arabia. Our goals shifted like the sand, next we were there to liberate Kuwait. Another goal was to remove Saddam as a military influence in the region. It's been said over and over but I have to say it again. The first casualty in war is truth.

What about that buffoon Willard Scott? I remember seeing him on TV giving the weather report from the gulf. He was wearing a desert brown camouflage uniform and carrying an M-16 rifle. No one bothered to tell him he was carrying the rifle backwards. Where'd he go once the shooting started? I wondered, what's he going to do with that rifle? Was he going to shoot someone from the National Weather Service or another network? Maybe he should stick to honoring the elders instead of trying to whip up patriotic fervor. I suppose it was a media ploy to get us used to seeing desert cammies.

We not only sent our children to the war but also our names. We had tomahawk cruise missiles and Apache, Kiowa, and Blackhawk helicopters in the war.

While the Gulf War was going on, I got together with a couple of Vietnam vets and we talked about things. First, we agreed no one can hate war as much as someone who has been in one. While talking, we discussed how to end war. One idea was to ban all sports until the hostilities cease. Think about it now, if your kid can't play hockey until the shooting stops, it would help make us aware that a war is going on. If Michael Jordan is earthbound for the duration, we would all be making a sacrifice for the war. No NFL, NBA, NHL, or spring training until people quit dying in the desert. Would Americans be willing to make such a sacrifice? I don't think so.

We veterans realize it is part of man's nature to make war. I suggest that no wars should be allowed until all the veterans of the previous one have died of old age. That would give us a few more years of peace instead of the way we do it now.

Here on the Rez, through the magic of television, we rode a few smart bombs to the targets and the war was over real quick. Who can ever forget those burning oil wells?

The country went crazy with yellow ribbons and flag

waving. I thought there were better ways to show support for the troops. I thought we could donate food for the hungry, help the houseless, visit an elder, teach someone to read, be a volunteer driver, donate blood, or something besides hanging those yellow ribbons that don't really mean anything.

The celebrations at the end of the Gulf War got real old real quick. The flag waving was overdone.

Near the Rez, the 109th Light Equipment Maintenance Company came home after five months in Saudi Arabia. According to one of the troops, all they did was sort mail and play volleyball. When they arrived there were signs proclaiming them as heroes.

Granted, living in tents in the desert was not very comfortable. It must have been tense with the thoughts of Scuds and gas warfare. I'm sure that many troops saw combat and were exposed to traumatic events but that doesn't make everyone a hero.

Stephen Bentzlin, the Lakota Marine who died in combat, comes closer to the word hero than a volleyball player.

I have a question for Americans over the age of thirty who go nuts waving ribbons and flags. Where were you when the warriors came home from the Vietnam War? A war that saw 58,000 killed in action. A war that caused over 60,000 of the veterans to kill themselves after the fighting was over. Tragic isn't it, more Vietnam veterans have killed themselves than actually died in the war?

In our rush to honor the brown-clad troops, we must remember those who wore green and died in larger numbers in Vietnam.

After the Gulf War there was a surplus of food that

was gathered for the conflict. The surplus food was given to Indian reservations and Russia.

At our house we were given a box of 2400 tea bags. The orange pekoe tea came in packages of one hundred tea bags. If we drank two cups a day, we would have enough for over three years. I hate to look a gift tea bag in the face but I prefer green tea anyway, just like my grandpa.

Rather than let the tea go to waste, we have redefined it. The tea bags are now officially called Desert Storm souvenirs. We give them out to visitors who may not have had a chance to pick up any souvenirs from the war.

One year my wife and I went to Washington, D.C., for the Marine Corps birthday and Veterans Day. The planning for this trip was easy—get to the airport and get on the right airplane.

I had a window seat and while looking out at the wing, I noticed a loose screw on top of the wing. It was sticking out about an inch. I had never seen that before so I told my wife who told the flight attendant. She looked at it and went back to her routine. It didn't look like she was looking for a screwdriver so we just settled down to watch the screw for the rest of the flight. Some other passengers overheard my wife tell the flight attendant about the screw so they helped watch too. There were even some people from the other side of the aisle who helped us watch the loose screw.

We walked away from that landing in Cleveland knowing it was our combined willpower, prayers, and good luck that had held the wing together. The connecting flight was uneventful. My favorite kind of airplane ride.

Patricia and I set up camp in a motel in D.C. After unpacking we went to a nice place and had a prime rib that was *thissssssss* big. There might have been someone famous in there but we didn't notice. We did notice the ferns in the windows kept us from seeing the street people outside.

After eating, we went to the Wall, the Vietnam Veterans Memorial. While there we talked with the living vets and honored the fallen.

The vets usually wear something that identifies them as participants in the Vietnam War. For some, it is a jungle uniform, complete down to the white, scuffed jungle boots. For others it is a Purple Heart pinned to a three-piece suit or a unit patch. Mostly, the veterans recognize one another by looking in one another's eyes.

There were veterans walking through the crowd searching for someone from their past. When they found someone, they hugged. There was a strong feeling of camaraderie among the proud, getting-old veterans.

Seeing the names etched on the Wall brought floods of memories and emotions. One feeling was the sense of loss. All of those dead men and women from the bayonet end of America's foreign policy. Another feeling was pride, just knowing that you had paid your dues to America by fighting in the war. Then there was the feeling of gratitude for having survived the experience, followed quickly by a feeling of guilt. When I found a name on the Wall I knew, I immediately remembered all of the circumstances of that marine's death. I could recall what the weather was like, where we were operating, and our mission. I dredged up memories of how they looked when we loaded them into the choppers. I touched every name I knew.

When we were done honoring the living and dead veterans, we went to the Smithsonian. One display that turned us off was the Columbus exhibit. There was a map that showed where Chris-what's-his-name landed. With the map was an Indian's skull. When we saw that, we left. My wife said we walked out like we were late for a bingo game.

As we taxied around, we could see most buildings had jailhouse bars over the windows and doors. After hearing about the six to twelve murders each day, we knew why the citizens locked themselves in jail at night.

On our last day in town, we went to Arlington Cemetery. We saw the graves of the brothers Kennedy. From there we walked to the Grandfather Plaque which was set up to honor Native American veterans. The cottonwood tree planted during the dedication is growing nicely. It is adorned with tobacco ties, eagle feathers, and other sacred things. It felt better standing there than it would have felt being in the Arlington amphitheater, where President Bush was talking about the Gulf War.

We watched the twenty-one measured paces of the soldier guarding the Tomb of the Unknown Soldier.

In a building near the tomb we saw a display case that held a coup stick and warbonnet belonging to Chief Plenty Coups of the Crow people. While we were looking at it, a cynical Vietnam vet said he saw the parents of the Unknown Soldier outside. We all dashed out to look before we realized what he had said.

We didn't get a chance to check the screws on the wing of the airplane that brought us home. It was too dark to see so we just held our breath during the flight back to Minnesota.

I am always interested in veterans' doings so when I heard a Vietnam Veteran Memorial would be dedicated in Duluth, I motored to the ceremony.

I was curious to see if Anishinaabeg would be represented or honored at this ceremony. We could see the WHITE monument as we approached the proceedings. There were approximately one thousand people there for the event. Most of the participants were WHITE although there were a few brown faces sprinkled in the crowd.

It was a typical WHITE guy ceremony with prayers, guitars, and a flyover by air force jets. Two Huey choppers went by at the end of the ceremony.

The huge, WHITE structure had been built by volunteers from the veteran and construction community. The WHITE monument is built in the shape of a half shell with bunkerlike windows overlooking Lake Superior.

The names of those killed in the Vietnam War are etched on a black stone wall.

There were flags everywhere. The WHITE honor guards, in their WHITE shirts, were standing on the WHITE concrete. WHITE seagulls flew around the crowd. Big, WHITE puffy clouds drifted by as the ceremony wound down. Two WHITE people keeled over from the heat or the emotion of the moment. They were assisted by WHITE soldiers of the local National Guard outfit.

The Duluth Mayor at the time, John Fedo, made some

forgettable remarks. I wondered who chose him to deliver a speech? I don't think he is a veteran.

In looking back at the dedication ceremony, I can only conclude that Anishinaabeg people were left out of the WHITE guy ceremony. We thought it was real WHITE of them to forget our contributions.

I read in the newspaper that another memorial was erected for Vietnam veterans in St. Paul. I didn't attend the ceremony. The design was chosen from among hundreds submitted. It is a silhouette of the state of Minnesota. Then-Governor Rudy Perpich promised to help raise funds for the construction.

Back in the '70s, we Vietnam veterans got a cash bonus from the State of Minnesota. My friends told me that then-Governor Perpich was responsible for getting us the bonus. I had a chance to talk with him and I thanked him for his work on behalf of the veterans. I asked if he would be interested to know what I did with my $600 bonus. He chuckled and said yes. I told him I spent $575 on wine, women, and song and just pissed the rest away. He smiled and quit shaking my hand. Rudy Perpich looked like he didn't really want to talk with me anymore.

Like some other Vietnam veterans, I'd like to say this about the Minnesota memorial:

"It's about #@&(%$()+$# time."

I thought the Reservation should give a cash bonus to their Vietnam veterans also. With the bulging coffers full of gambling gold, they could afford to give the thirty-some Fonjalackers who fought in that war a bonus. I suggested it to the Reservation Business Committee but it fell on deaf ears.

In August of 1995, I went to Washington, D.C., for a

reunion. Grunts from India Company, Third Battalion, Ninth Marines, Third Marine Division got together again.

The patrol base was set up in a plush Arlington, Virginia, hotel. The perimeter was set up in the hospitality suite. There was a sign-up sheet by the front entrance of the suite. Almost every grunt coming through the door looked at the list of names.

We looked at helmets, slides, pictures, maps, flags, the flak jackets and jungle boots. But mostly, we looked at each other's eyes. The feeling of being with a brother was there again. I saw three grunts pushing at each other to see who would have the privilege of pushing a disabled vet's wheelchair.

The mud marines of India Company were in a difficult place to do a difficult job. I learned some Indian Company history while in the hospitality suite. Six months after I'd left Vietnam, a platoon leader from my company was awarded the Medal of Honor. Lt. John Bobo gave his life for his men and his country.

Seeing and talking with the grunts caused the memories to come flooding back. We were young, strong, and thought we were bulletproof. Each dead marine we loaded on a helicopter took part of that bulletproof feeling away. We used to tell ourselves bad things happened to the other guy, but I used to wonder when it would be my turn to take a one-way chopper ride. At the time, I was more worried about getting wounded than getting killed. Our attitude at the time was—if it moves, shoot it. If it doesn't move, burn it. Now I know why we were called the Flaming I. The first part of the directions used to locate us in the field went something like this—"Do you see all that smoke? Well, that is where India Company is operating today."

During the war I was more concerned with mundane matters like: How far do we have to walk today? Will the choppers be able to make it in to deliver ammo, water, and food? When the choppers couldn't come in because of the weather or enemy fire, we'd get hungry. Then we'd play little games, like "Do you remember what mashed potatoes taste like? What about blueberry pie and ice cream? Can you picture the taste, smell, and sound when you bite into an apple?"

We were living on a diet of C-rations. I learned to like them, though a lot of Marines didn't. When the choppers couldn't come in to resupply, I still had food. I went to Vietnam weighing 180 pounds; after thirteen months of C-rations, I weighed 130.

During the war, my overriding thought was about water. There always seemed to be a shortage of good drinking water. Sometimes we drank from the rice paddies. I used to try to imagine a tall glass of ice water. I could almost see the water beading up on the outside of the glass, ice cubes clinking. The water I imagined was so cold, it gave me a forehead headache to think about it. I remember thinking a lot about water during my time in the war.

India Company went everywhere together during the reunion in Washington, D.C. We went to the Wall together. Names, so many names of our friends. Another part of the patrol was a trip to the Iwo Jima Memorial. I looked up at the statue and thought of Ira Hayes, a

Pima Indian who is depicted in the statue. Another Indian marine, I thought.

In Vietnam, the grunts rode on tanks, amtracs, and in choppers. This time we were riding in an air-conditioned bus. It was cushy.

The patrol continued to Marine Barracks, Washington, D.C. Every marine knows what 8th and I Street means. It is the top of the chain of command. The commandant of the Marine Corps sleeps there.

The Silent Drill Team was impressive. Twenty-four marines doing the same thing at the same time. The old grunts sat up a little straighter when the drill team came marching by.

The music from the band stirred us. When they played "The Marine's Hymn," we all jumped to our feet and stood at attention. We left with the sound of "Taps" still in our ears. The bus ride back to the hotel was quiet.

The last patrol was at the banquet. The grunts ate together like they did some twenty-five to thirty years ago. We told war stories over and over. It was different telling war stories with these vets. When we were talking about getting mortared or ambushed, we were talking about the very same incident. At each table, grunts from India Company promised to see each other again. Some grunts got up and thanked those responsible for making the reunion happen. It was kind of funny when the DJ suddenly made a loud noise with his sound equipment. Every grunt in the room ducked, some more than others.

The DJ played music from our time in the war. While some danced with their wives, others continued telling stories. We knew we were helping each other heal from the Vietnam War.

On the drive back to Sawyer, Minnesota, I had plenty of time to reflect on what had happened in the previous five days. All in all, it was a good time but there were some bad parts too.

It was good seeing the faces of the guys I knew but I couldn't help but wondering about all the marines I didn't see. Were they dead? I could also see some of the vets at the reunion were still troubled by their memories.

As for me, I had nightmares again for a couple of weeks after I came home. At first it was scary but I was soon sleeping through the night again. I think that is part of the price of being a veteran. It takes a lot more than honor songs at a powwow to heal that kind of hurt. I suggested to the readers of my column that they should hug the next vet they see.

I still enjoy celebrating Veterans Day. When I first wake up on Veterans Day mornings, I stand at the position of attention and salute all veterans of all wars. Then I sit down and have a tall glass of ice water. Veterans Day always reminds me of parades.

When I was young, I used to go to parades in downtown Duluth. This was before television so a parade was big doings. The music from the bands, the soldiers marching and flags fluttering all added to the excitement. For me, one highlight of those 1950s Duluth parades was waiting for this one real old man.

His name was Albert Woolson and he was identified as the last surviving member of the Grand Army of the Republic. He had fought for the Union in the Civil War.

When I saw him, he wasn't doing much of anything. I don't remember him waving to the crowd, all he was doing was smiling and riding along.

I waved at him though. I knew I was looking at a

piece of living American history. This man was alive when Abe Lincoln was president. He had fought in a war I read about in my school's history books.

Later on as an adult, I wondered about him and his long life. Did he read a newspaper that reported the hanging of thirty-eight Dakota in Mankato, Minnesota, during Christmas week of 1862? Where was he when General Custer met Sitting Bull, Gall, and Crazy Horse? Was he in Minnesota when Anishinaabeg warriors drove off the Fort Snelling troops at Sugar Point? Was he shocked when the Lakota were slaughtered at Wounded Knee? Did he have children or grandchildren in the Spanish-American War? What did he really think of World Wars I and II?

That old man was a veteran of war and life.

I became a veteran after my time in Vietnam. We didn't get a parade. Instead, we got blamed for losing an unpopular war. We were the visible symbol of the failure of America's policies. I remembered how some veterans returned their medals to the U. S. government. I heard about other veterans getting spit on by American citizens after their return from Vietnam.

Life was too difficult for some who came home after the war. Veterans killed themselves at an ugly rate. Lewis Puller, Jr., son of marine legend Chesty Puller, ended his life with a shotgun. He was severely wounded in Vietnam, wrote a Pulitzer prize-winning book about it, then died.

That particular tragedy also struck my family. We buried a brother after a car accident. Rod Northrup was killed in the accident but died from what is now called Post Traumatic Stress Disorder.

I believe Vietnam veterans should be looked on as examples of the strength of the human spirit. They endured and survived Vietnam and its aftermath.

But once again my peers are dying. This time it isn't enemy gunfire that is killing them. Suicide isn't taking so many anymore. What is killing them now is the awful legacy of Agent Orange.

I went to Richard Arredondo's funeral at Fort Snelling. He was a Dakota relative, a Vietnam veteran. He left his wife and children much too early. The color guard fired their rifles and then "Taps" was played. The sound of the mournful music bounced off the rows of white tombstones. I saluted at the end like the other veterans. A grateful nation gave an American flag to the family.

When that was over the Dakota people said good-bye to one of their warriors. Richard had made a claim against the government because of his exposure to Agent Orange. The claim was denied and his appeal was pending when he died of lymphoma.

The Fond du Lac Reservation honored their Vietnam vets in 1996 by holding a powwow in Sawyer. The living and dead veterans were remembered by the Reservation and its people. Chairman Robert Peacock, a Vietnam vet, spoke to the assembled vets and family members. Honor songs were sung, the drums were heard and felt.

The Reservation Business Committee gave the veterans gifts. As a vet, I got an eagle feather, sage wrapped with the colors of the Vietnam Campaign ribbon, a knife, a clock, a calculator, a Reservation flag, a couple of T-shirts, and a shiny black jacket with Fond du Lac's symbol on the back.

During the honoring ceremony, two F-16 Fighting

Falcons jets from the 148th Air National Guard flew over. My sister, Doris Smith, said she became emotional and almost cried during that part of the ceremony. She remembered her brothers and cousins who fought in the Vietnam War.

The jets were five minutes late according to the schedule used by the powwow planning committee. A vet said the jets were sometimes late in Vietnam also.

The Vietnam veterans talked among themselves and told war stories. The powwow grounds were littered with imaginary grenade pins and empty C-ration cans when the vets were done telling stories. There was a feast and veterans were fed first. They didn't have to stand in the line that was hundreds of people long.

It is a good idea to honor veterans but a better idea is to quit making them. Our young men and women are still scattered all over the world facing danger. My television is still teaching me about new places: Grenada, Lebanon, Panama, Somalia, Iraq, Bosnia.

Albert Woolson, that old veteran of the Civil War, is gone now. I've decided I want his job. I want to ride in a parade as the last surviving veteran of the Vietnam War.

Gambling and Other Follies

ATAAGEWIN

I DON'T KNOW what we did with all of our time and money before we got bingo halls and casinos.

The word gaming is used by the governments—tribal, state, and federal—to describe what we are doing at the bingo halls and casinos. It sounds too polite to my ears. I call it gambling.

The Anishinaabeg have been gambling for centuries. The moccasin game was one of our early forms of gambling. It is still played in the summer at powwows. Now we have bingo, blackjack, and slot machines at our casinos. My Reservation owns two of them. One in Carlton, Minnesota, called the Black Bear and the other in Duluth, called Fond du Luth. Gambling started off small on this Reservation. In the beginning there was bingo, then we grew into casinos. The history of our entry into the gambling market is full of numbers and dates.

In 1989, Big Bucks Bingo announced a profit of $369,000 for the previous year. The money was used to pay the bills for our failed furnace factory. Business guru

Scott Fisher says we can go into another business now that the bills are paid.

The Reservation Business Committee used bingo money to purchase land. In 1985, they bought part of a city block in downtown Duluth. The land was put into Trust status and became part of the Reservation. They also purchased a parcel of 350 acres near the intersection of Highway 210 and Interstate 35.

In September of 1990, I had reservations about the Reservation's plan for gambling. I was reserved because I had seen so many sins committed in the name of economic development. The Reservation planners told the people what they had in mind. They had big plans for the new bingo hall, the 36-bed motel, a 150-seat restaurant, a culture center, a museum and education center, a gas station and convenience store. Nature trails, cross country ski trails, an amphitheater, and individually owned shops are all on the drawing board.

The planners estimated the overall cost would be eight to ten million dollars.

In May of 1991, the Reservation added slot machines to the bingo hall offerings. At first, it was a tiny addition to the Ojibwe School gymnasium. The bingo game evolved into slot machines and blackjack and then they needed more room. The former furnace factory became a casino. It was just a temporary casino until the big one was built near the Interstate.

The Indians began forming associations and I stopped by to visit the First Annual Traditional National Indian Gaming Convention. The doings were held at a ritzy hotel in Bloomington, Minnesota.

We saw suits and braids at the convention, sometimes the same person was wearing both. The Fond du Lac

Rez was well represented at the get-together. We saw employees from the accounting division, legal, planning, administration, the Rez newspaper, and band government.

There were a lot of video gambling machines on display at the convention. Security was tight, only those with convention badges were allowed in the display area. I borrowed a badge and looked at the machines. I learned that the machines can be set to a certain pay-back percentage.

I saw two famous Indians at the convention. Floyd Red Crow Westerman, singer and actor, was there. I talked about the old boarding school days with Floyd. He attended Flandreau Boarding School with some of my older cousins. The second famous one was Charlie Hill, comedian. He talked about a special he had just finished for Fox TV.

As I was leaving, I wondered what the odds are on having the Second Annual Traditional National Indian Gaming Convention in Minnesota?

Back at the Reservation, we were painfully learning how to manage a casino. One marketing gimmick became known as white people per capita payments. The RBC claims losses of only $100,000. We think they lost twice as much.

Here's the way it worked. A person would buy a coupon book for twenty dollars. Inside the book were five coupons worth twenty dollars each. That comes out to an eighty dollar profit per book for the buyer. It was mostly white people that took advantage of the limited offer. The Shinnobs didn't hear of it or couldn't afford the initial twenty dollars.

The Reservation Business Committee claimed they

didn't know anything about the marketing gimmick. They pointed the finger at the former casino manager who had left some months before. The former casino manager, Mike Walsh, called me to explain his part of the coupon deal. The marketing plan was formalized after he left. The coupon books were sitting at the casino for weeks before they were released. He did accept part of the blame for the check cashing firm that went belly up, owing the Reservation $100,000. He thought it was a straight business deal. Fond du Lac was not the only victim; Walsh named other Indian casinos that had used the same check cashing firm. Walsh repeatedly denied any knowledge of the coupon book deal. Now I don't know who to believe. The Reservation Business Committee wouldn't lie to me, would they?

I stopped in the interim casino and saw over one hundred people standing in line to get their free money. I pointed out the money leak to the worried looking casino manager. He told me it was a long story. I thought it should be a long story for that much money.

The Reservation Business Committee does sometimes give something to the Rez people. In a burst of Christmas cheer, the RBC gave everyone a ham. Casino workers, Rez employees, and Fonjalackers got part of the pig. The RBC didn't actually handle the gift. They created a coupon that could be redeemed for a ham at the B & B Market in Cloquet. There were quite a few cars lined up when I stopped to get my ham.

At the risk of looking a gift pig in the snout, my ham was mostly fat. After I cut away the artery-clogging fat, I had enough meat for two tiny sandwiches. I bet there was enough fat in the fifteen hundred hams to waterproof all of the boots in the Chinese Army.

My cousin, Rathide, says the RBC is taking care of us. Instead of giving out dirty, old, gambling per capita money, they are giving us the food directly. Yah, they put the pork to us.

With this much good luck, we wonder if something bad is going to happen. We're hoping the new Black Bear Casino, just off the Interstate, is a success. Maybe next year we'll get a dozen eggs to go with the ham.

Planning for the new casino continues. At one RBC meeting, I learned the new seven-million-dollar casino will now cost fourteen million dollars. Another funny story from the moccasin telegraph reports how one leader, not from Fond du Lac, handled the strain. It may or may not be true, we are waiting for details. This is the version we heard:

The leader from a gambling tribe was feeling the burdens of office and was drinking alcohol to relieve the tensions. The leader drank for several hours in a liquor store just off his Rez. After a while, the leader got a call from nature. It was the kind that a person has to answer.

While sitting on the throne in the bathroom, the leader fell asleep and tipped over. One never knows when a nap will sneak up when alcohol is involved. The leader was on the floor in public view, with pants at half mast. It was said the leader was either showing there was nothing to hide or what happens when you drink too much, maybe signaling a new openness in government.

Two Rez residents helped cover the situation as they helped their leader get upright and presentable.

This leader is responsible for decisions affecting hundreds of people and millions of gambling dollars. The voters could do themselves a favor and flush this one out of office at the next election.

The Bear is up and running. Band Chairman Sonny Peacock calls the Black Bear Casino an economic shot in the arm for the Fond du Lac Reservation and the surrounding community. Ojibwe speakers call it *Makade Makwa*—Black Bear.

The fifteen- to eighteen-million dollar (estimates vary) casino had what Peacock seductively called a soft opening.

The chairman is betting millions that the customers will pour off the freeway to pour millions into the slot machines. The machines made a pleasant *boing, boing* sound as people bet their money. *Boing, boing,* more money for Fond du Lac, boing, boing, more money for Fond du Lac. While gazing around at the gamblers, I noticed most of them had gray hair, sort of like that bumper sticker that says, "We're spending our children's inheritance." What my cousin, Rathide, calls the Ben Gay crowd.

The fact that the Bear is wholly owned by the Rez means we won't be splitting money with an outside management company. Peacock said any Fonjalacker can get a job there.

I have a long list of relatives working at the Bear. Two sisters, my son Matthew, a couple of nieces and nephews, and a lot of cousins are cashing paychecks from the casino. My oldest son, Jim, helped build the place. The steady paychecks let them pay their bills, maybe gamble at another casino.

The new gambling started with a U.S. Supreme Court

decision involving Indians from California and Florida. The decision allowed Indian tribes to raise their bingo limits above what state law allows. Fond du Lac was one of the first with high stakes bingo in Minnesota.

I don't brag about it or put it on my resume but I was one of the first gambling employees hired by the Rez. At first, I sold bingo boards to the players. Chips were used to mark the numbers called. I wore a white carpenter's nail apron to hold my change. After a while, I moved up in the ranks and became a bingo caller. One night, my wife Patricia couldn't get to sleep. She was tossing, turning, and shaking the bed. I asked her to lie still so I could get to sleep. When she continued rolling around the bed, I started crooning, "Under the B-7, B number seven . . . I-16, I, one six . . . N-39, N three nine . . . G-46, G four six . . ."

And so on until she fell asleep. It took one regular and one special game before I could get back to sleep.

I sure enjoyed being a bingo caller. What power. I could make the whole hall go silent by saying, "Your first number is . . ."

I would have fun with the numbers as I called them. Some numbers developed slang names. For example, I would say, "Under the B-11, B chicken legs, or N-44, N Dolly Parton, or G-57, Heinz 57, or Colt 45, or Under the Highway 61. For all you young lovers—O-69."

I would rock the ball back and forth on the camera that was linked to monitors in the bingo hall. I think the old ladies liked it, I never got any complaints. A bingo player came up to me after the game and said, "You never call my numbers."

"I don't know what your numbers are," I told her.

She then gave me her telephone number.

How could you tell they liked to play bingo?

Their dog was named Dauber, their kids were
called Early Bird, Postage Stamp, Four Corners,
and Blackout.

What four words do bingo players hate?

Someone else already won.

What's a new Ojibwe word for bingo?

Juremawwin? (Did your mother win?)

What's a new Ojibwe word for casino?

Jurepawin? (Did your father win?)

Gambling has done a lot for us in the last decade.
For one thing, it has brought our Rez unemployment
rate from 80 percent all the way down to 50 percent.

What is the unemployment rate on the Rez?

I don't know, that's not my job.

Gambling has given us economic clout. I don't think
the banker puts our leaders on hold when they call to
talk business.

Gambling is creating a new stereotype, however. This
is the idea that all of us are getting rich from the casino
profits. Actually, only a small percentage of us get

money from gambling. So far, each enrolled Fonjalacker gets an annual per capita payment of fifteen hundred dollars. At this rate, it won't be long before I can get that red Italian sports car, maybe even send my grandchildren to Harvard or Yale—no, buy a condo in Vail or Aspen. I get dizzy when I try to crunch numbers that big.

Each Reservation decides how to spend its gambling profits. Some people get a lot of money and some don't. I think it is creating a class-based society. I can tell who is getting a huge per capita check by looking in the parking lots at powwows. The ones driving a 32-foot Winnebago with two air conditioners and a satellite dish are the per capita Indians. The ones sleeping on the ground in tents are not getting money from their casinos. Personally, I think we need things to bring us together rather than separate us.

We frequently read in the newspaper how white people steal from their employers to gamble at Indian casinos. Thus, a new legal defense is born.

"Blame the Indians, it was their casino that made me steal."

At our local casino, a white customer wouldn't accept change given to her by my cousin. She didn't want to touch the money the Indians had handled. As an Anishinaabe, walking around the casino, I think it's funny that people think all Indians are employees of the casino. One day I had to give directions to the restroom three times before I could get my first quarter in a slot machine.

What's the player's responsibility at the casino?

To move the coins from one slot machine to another.

Why did he go to the casino every night?

To prove he wasn't a compulsive gambler.

What's the difference between a gambler and a compulsive gambler?

Like drunks and alcoholics, one of them has to go to meetings, I bet.

The Reservation Business Committee went from administering federally subsidized programs to running a multimillion-dollar business enterprise. They learned about labor problems during the first lean winter.

"Regrettably for economic reasons, it is necessary to lay off a number of employees. This letter is to inform you that you are among those affected."

That was the beginning of a letter sent to sixty employees of the Black Bear Casino. Over half of those laid off were Shinnobs.

The former employees began meeting at the Sawyer Community Center to talk about the event. In sometimes angry tones, the people shared their problems.

One employee was told that the layoff was for two weeks, another was told two months. The laid-off employees were confused and the Shinnobs met with the Reservation Business Committee. In a three-hour meeting, RBC members explained what caused the layoffs. Chairman Sonny Peacock said the customer base wasn't there. He also explained the point system that was used to decide who would be laid off.

The point system is a new management tool that takes points off for different reasons. The policy was made retroactive to when the employee first started. Some people had points taken away for attending funerals, others for being sick.

A worker told the chairman that she had been sent home because the casino wasn't busy. This was counted as an unexcused absence using the point system.

Secretary-Treasurer Pete Defoe said he thought the people were treated unfairly and said his job is to see that the people get their jobs back. He told the assembled Shinnobs that their complaints would not be ignored.

A Shinnob still working at the casino reported a new memo, which stated that anyone talking about the layoffs would get three days off or be terminated.

Chairman Peacock couldn't answer when asked how many Shinnobs were working at the casino. He said each case would be reviewed by the RBC. He told the people to come back the next day if they wanted their jobs.

The next day the people showed up, but the RBC members were away attending other meetings. They did leave one RBC member behind who explained how the employees could get their layoffs reviewed.

The people were angry and decided to picket the casino. Some brave souls showed up carrying signs that said, "Will work for food."

I think the local TV news crews helped decide policy on the layoffs. Most of those laid off went back to work after the casino picket line.

The Rez goes through casino managers like rolls of toilet paper. Elwin Benton, Fonjalacker, is now gone from the casino. Two other Fonjalackers are now handling the administrative duties. Mike Himango and Jerry Savage are the co-managers. Some might find fault with these management problems but considering how other casinos do it, I think we should continue looking inside to find casino managers. As the old saying goes, you gotta kiss a lot of frogs to find a prince.

I know other casinos pay up to 40 percent of their revenues for white guys to come in and manage their operations. I think we are better off making our own mistakes.

What was life like on the Reservations before gambling? Let's go back and take a look.

In 1980, Shinnobs were facing discrimination and prejudice on a daily basis. Bigots were everywhere. The towns around the Reservation were the worst for racism. I called it a "hate circle" around the Rez.

Most Americans were not aware of the problems we faced every day. Their view of us was a mix of twentieth-century Hollywood and nineteenth-century idealism. Some people were surprised that we were still here. We learned how to survive and even flourish in spite of the racism. We continued to teach our children how to live in a racist society.

The system's tentacles reached deeper into our lives than those of any other population group. Once a Shinnob got wrapped up, it was difficult to escape. We were not people, we were clients, patients, or inmates. Sometimes we were lumped together and called a caseload.

The probation officer talked to the judge who talked to the police who talked to the lawyer who talked to the social worker who talked to the counselor who talked to the child protection worker who talked to the probation officer. Shinnobs enmeshed in the system rarely got away without losing their dignity, their freedom, or their children.

Jails always held more than their share of Shinnobs. The sentences seemed to be longer and the punishments more severe. A jury of their peers was a joke. I couldn't name one Shinnob who ever served on a jury even if you held a bayonet against my throat. The only Shinnobs in the courtroom either wore connected steel bracelets or were called defendants. Going to jail was considered normal and not an aberration. There were many family reunions held in the cell blocks. Shinnobs were 1 percent of the population of Minnesota but made up 25 percent of the jail and prison populations. It was tough being a free Indian in those days.

Schools added to the problem by labeling most Shinnobs as learning disabled. Once a label was applied, it was difficult to remove. In school, the students learned that they were "discovered" and were a "conquered people." They also learned about the wisdom of the white man with no mention of their own contributions.

White students were especially cruel to the Shinnobs. My son, Joseph, told me it doesn't feel good to be called a dirty Indian in class. Some schools used Indians as mascots, something less than human. It was a challenging test to be an Indian in the schools then. It is no surprise that most students quit school before graduation.

Foster homes and adoption agencies did a brisk business in Indian children. The Shinnobs were taken from their families at an alarming rate. We also learned a new word: dysfunctional. The word meant someone else was going to raise your children. It was sad to watch these born-Shinnob-raised-white people returning to the Reservation. We helped them find their identity that was taken by the system. It was hard to even remain Indian back in the '80's.

Shinnobs exercising their treaty rights were arrested by game wardens and harassed by white people. Wild rice, deer meat, ducks, and fish were confiscated by the game wardens. Canoes, nets, and guns were also taken away. Each arrest and confiscation was a reminder of how the United States kept its word in the treaties. People still continued to exercise their rights in spite of threats, gunfire, and bombs. They were the only ones who believed in the words of the treaties. It was hard to be a treaty believing Indian in the 1980s.

Back in the bad old days, tribal governments were trying to qualify for federal and private grants. Job training programs blossomed and then withered. A lot of us learned a little about a lot of different occupations. On my Rez, we had welders, carpenters, heavy equipment operators, natural resources technicians, and electronics workers. We followed the Golden Rule in those days—those with the gold make the rules. Washington and foundation dollars ruled the reservations with their policies. Tribal governments were just learning to flex their economic muscles.

Here it is the '90s and little has changed except the calendar. We are still facing racism, personal and institutional, every day. But there is one difference, the tribal governments have control of the gambling gold.

What's the difference between praying in church and praying at the casino?

At the casino, you really mean it.

What do you say to people leaving the casino?

Miigwech, giiwe naadin nawaj zhooniyaa. (Thanks, go home and get more money.) Or to put it another way, *Miigwetch, umbe gewe aindahyin chi-nagi bahtwadamin nahwuge zhooniyaas.* (Thanks, go home and get more money.)

I have heard that gambling is called the new "buffalo" for the Indian people. I disagree with that comparison. I think gambling is a tiger. Riding a tiger is exciting, but how do we get off?

I get excited when I go to the bingo hall and am waiting for one number. My heart thumps a little faster when the last seven falls into place on the slot machine. Exciting.

Donald Trump testified to Congress that Indian casinos are ripe for a takeover by organized crime. He said the mob has already infiltrated Indian casinos. However, he could offer no proof other than that people are talking about it.

Here on the Fond du Lac Reservation, we don't have to worry about organized crime; it is the unorganized crime we have to be concerned about. As with any new, large, evolving organization, we have had some problems. We don't have an outside management group so we make all our own mistakes. We have had some big dollar mistakes. That check cashing firm got away with hundreds of thousands of dollars. The RBC loaned them the money because they were having a problem with cash flow. I heard they told our leaders the check was in the mail just before they went bankrupt. We are having expensive growing pains as we enter the gambling market.

The original agreement that allowed us to open a casino in downtown Duluth is another prime example. The Rez had a successful bingo hall operating and the Reservation Business Committee decided to expand the market. They bought an old abandoned building in Duluth and poured in megabucks to turn the former Sears store into a gambling casino. The land was put into Trust Status and now we have part of the Reservation in downtown Duluth.

According to the original agreement with the city, the profits are split as follows: 25 percent to the Rez, 25 percent to the city, and the remaining 50 percent was to be given to the Joint Economic Development Commission. We were wondering why we are giving part of the profits to Duluth since it is our sovereignty, our money, that made the casino happen.

Duluth and the Reservation are trying to decide how to split the millions that have built up. Instead of creating a harmonious relationship, they have become adversaries. I expect one side or the other to make a federal case out of it. The National Indian Gaming Commission agreed with us and decreed that we should be getting 70 percent instead of 25 percent of the profits. The Fond du Luth Casino was reporting profits of seven million dollars annually.

One of the major reasons given for creating a casino in Duluth was the promise of jobs. Whenever I go to that casino, all I see are white people working. If this is an Indian casino, where are the Indians?

The gambling tiger doesn't care who it eats. We had an accountant here on the Reservation who stole more than $60,000 of our money. He was a trusted employee for almost ten years. His gambling addiction caused him troubles when he wrote Reservation checks to himself. His reputation and career were sacrificed to the tiger.

More recently, the area director of the Bureau of Indian Affairs, Earl Barlow, was suspended because he accepted gambling vouchers from one of the casinos he was regulating. His assistant was also suspended. That's two more careers consumed by the gambling tiger.

Those are two of the highly publicized cases. We constantly read in the newspapers about people who steal from their employers to feed the gambling tiger. We are wondering who will be corrupted by the tiger next?

The Reservation Business Committee spends a lot of time, brainpower, and money on gambling. Our chairman, Sonny Peacock, recently estimated that he spends a third of his time on gambling issues. I think his estimate is low. I bet it is 50 percent or more.

Gambling begets greed. The gambling tiger is making us forget who we are as people. Everything is now measured in dollars.

I don't think gambling contributes to racial harmony either. Since the casino always wins, there are more losers walking out than winners. I can just about picture the losers saying, "Those God damned Indians got all my money again."

Since the experience is negative, I don't see how they can think positively about us. I worry that we are becoming full-blooded members of the rat race.

In my years on this earth, one of the things I have learned is that people will argue about money better than anything.

Here on the Fond du Lac Reservation, we are doing

something very unusual. It is unusual because we have never had to think about things like this.

We have to decide what to do with the millions of dollars we get from gambling.

We're breaking another stereotype here. Indians are supposed to be poor. Isn't that in the Constitution someplace, isn't it written that Indians gotta be poor? We are supposed to have what author Vine Deloria has called a plight.

People who have millions of dollars in the bank do not have a plight. They have problems deciding what to do with the money. The casino profits are building up. Just a few years ago, we were deciding between USDA commodity pork or chicken for supper. Commods were used to stave off starvation before gambling profits came to the Rez. Now we are in the world of high finance, running with the big dogs, as my cousin says.

At one meeting with the people, the RBC learned the people like to argue about money. I didn't go but heard they called the chairman everything but a chipmunk. His ancestry was questioned also.

There are many choices available on what to do with the money. We learned in a recent referendum that the people don't want to spend money for a new school building.

Some people want to cut up the profit pie and distribute it equally among all the members of the Fond du Lac Band of Lake Superior Chippewa, our formal, federal name. They want a per capita payment. I think there are problems with that idea. First of all, we would be overrun with people claiming to be $\frac{3}{5}$ or $\frac{19}{64}$ths Fonjalacker on their mother's side. We used to call such people Woodwork Indians. They come crawling out of the woodwork when the Indian pie is being cut up. Another cloud is the tax man. How much would we have to give to the federal government in taxes? As we know, the feds have got to have their cut.

The ancient cry of economic development is heard. Some say we should use the money to go into other business ventures. Diversify away from gambling because we don't know how long our monopoly will last. Lest we forget, we have had some bad experiences with a furnace factory and an electronic assembly workshop.

Others want to buy land. I remember that Will Rogers said something like, "Invest in land, they're not making any more." I like that idea. We use the white man's money to buy back our land that was stolen in the first place. There is something ironic about it. What a worthy goal—to be able to say we own most of the Reservation. At least 51 percent anyway. If we do it gradually, buy a little at a time, the owners won't jack up the prices. We could make a long-range plan to own the whole Reservation in two hundred years, just a few generations down the line.

Why do you call it a Rez instead of a Reservation?

Because the white man owns most of it.

Still others want to augment the existing programs. The clinics in Cloquet and Duluth can always use money somewhere. Maybe they could add to the services they already provide. Perhaps expand that stop-smoking program, the one that uses those nicotine patches. My cousin, Rathide, was a failure at that program. Couldn't keep the patch lit, he says.

The Wild Rice Committee could use money to improve the Reservation watershed. That project has been operating on a small scale for a few years. Shinnobs who rice have been clearing the ditches of fallen trees to improve the water flow. They can use money to expand the project so the coming generations of Fonjalackers will have *manoomin.*

The Fond du Lac Community College has needs that are not met by existing funding sources. Gambling money could be used to educate Fond du Lac band members.

Programs for the elders, programs for the young ones. There are so many good ideas for the use of the money. Someone has got us all talking about money. While all of our attention is focused on that issue, what else is happening that we should know about?

The best way to settle this weighty question is to let the people decide when they vote. We vote every two years now for positions on the RBC. Just make it a continuing part of the ballot. How should we spend our money?

Everyone would win. The RBC would get a clear mandate from the people about the gambling profits. They would know where to put their energy. The people would win because they would be experiencing pure democracy.

We should decide quickly so we can quit talking about money. We should be talking about racism, fighting for clean air and water, protecting treaty rights, and preserving the language our elders spoke. Some things are more important than money.

I worry about what gambling is doing to us as people. Gambling is all about greed. I know one of the things that helped us survive on this continent for thousands of generations has been our willingness to share, the feeling that being generous is good. The idea that the community is more important than the individual. Gambling is just the opposite of that. Where will we be after twenty years of gambling? Thirty?

In spite of the problems associated with gambling, I still smile inside when I see white people at the casino reaffirming tribal sovereignty one quarter at a time, *boing boing.*

We're Still Here

NIMBWAAWINANICOO IN

WE'RE STILL HERE. The Anishinaabeg of the Fond du Lac Reservation, numbering about thirty-two hundred people, are here and living in the sea of America. As I travel about I am reminded of the differences and similarities.

Sometimes I think the white man was put here to amuse us. Some of the things they do or say make me laugh. They often make me want to cry too. One that cracked me up lately was this new ad campaign.

Now my TV tells me I need to buy a new kind of food for the cat. It is designed for the cat's urinary tract. I didn't even know I was supposed to be worried about cat pee. The ever-vigilant manufacturers and ad agencies have enlightened me and I now realize the error of my ways.

Jeez, another addition to the list of things I have to worry about.

Let's see now: Prairie Island killer waste, acid rain, the clear cutting of Minnesota, Wisconsin mining at

Crandon, unsafe drinking water, ravaged rain forests, and ozone holes.

Also war, racism, poverty, injustices, rent-a-shamans, treaty rights, crime, gambling, and a Rez car that won't start.

I'll have to drop one worry from the list to make room for the cat pee problems. I also have another worry, I don't have a cat. I'll have to get one so I can buy that new cat food designed for the cat's urinary tract. What will that white man think of next?

In a related note, I discovered that I can now buy bottled water for dogs.

As I travel about I constantly find reminders that the white man is trying to make me laugh. I was traveling near Galesburg, Illinois, and I found a new way of doing things.

The people in that area of the United States have invented self-sanding roads. Here is the way it works. In the fall, the farmers plow the cornfields. The wind blows the topsoil across the roads. It is all automatic—plow and then drive safely all winter because the roads are sanded. I never would have thought of that.

In the Upper Peninsula of Michigan, the white people call themselves Yoopers. As I was passing through Michigan one trip, I discovered a new technological breakthrough in outside toilets. They invented what is called a Yooper Two Holer outside toilet. In this variation, one hole is directly above the other. I didn't stay long enough to see who gets to be on top.

Of course, not all the white man's ideas make me laugh. The most recent one by Northern States Power almost made me cry. NSP has a plan to store radioactive wastes in dry casks. The casks would be placed on an island on the Mississippi River.

The utility has mounted an intense ad campaign to convince us it is okay to keep killer wastes at Prairie Island, home of the Mdewakanton. I saw expensive full-page ads in the newspapers, NSP people talking in soundbites for TV. They need this new plan because their storage pools are full and the plant will have to shut down. The only way to keep the nuclear power plant operating is by creating new storage sites for the killer waste.

The Minnesota legislature must approve of the new plans and they are debating the storage question. The vote was yes and no in various committees. Now they are talking compromise. Personally, I don't think it is possible to compromise with killer wastes. We need to quit making things that are dangerous for ten thousand years.

NSP says the storage is temporary until a permanent repository is built by the federal government. Earthquake prone Yucca Mountain, Nevada, has been suggested as one place to store the spent fuel rods.

The Mescalero Apache are flirting with the idea of building a private storage site for radioactive wastes. The storage site would be private because the state of New Mexico is against the idea. Some of the Apaches are opposed to the private storage site on their Reservation.

The idea of storing killer wastes on a Mississippi floodplain flies in the face of logic. We have not fully recovered from what was called a Once-in-a-Hundred-Years flood. We don't know where we are in the cycle of floods. We could be just a few years away from a Once-in-a-Thousand-Years flood.

If there is a larger flood next year, I can just about picture the steel casks clanging together as they float downstream. Maybe something heavy would float down and bang into the casks.

I am not anti-electricity. Electricity came to our part of the Rez in the 1950s. I can remember the first time I turned on a switch to get light. Gone were the days of the kerosene lamps. No more wick trimming, chimney cleaning. I didn't have to fill the lamps with pungent-smelling kerosene, just flip a switch.

At first, we used to just listen to the radio. I tell my kids, we didn't have TV so we had to sit around and watch the radio. Eventually we got television sets.

I watched the atom bomb tests on TV. I imagined myself as one of the soldiers climbing out of the trenches, advancing toward the mushroom-shaped clouds. Now, my TV tells me those same soldiers are filing claims against the government because of their exposure to radioactivity. The atomic veterans believed the government when it said it was safe. Now the government would have us believe the dry cask storage idea is safe also.

When the state legislature was talking compromise, one idea was to store the killer wastes in northern Minnesota. It was said that the geological formations in this area are ideal for storing the spent fuel rods. I have a message for the decision makers: Don't even think of it. We are upstream from everyone here. A nuclear accident here would poison everyone's water.

I wish the Department of Energy would listen to my plan for storing killer wastes. Put the spent fuel rods in the backyards of those who were responsible for making them. Make storage a family legacy. When the original responsible person dies, the wastes could stay in the family, year after year until they are safe. The experts say it would only take ten thousand years, maybe twenty-four thousand years.

Northern States Power executives, state legislators, and federal agency heads could document the safety of dry cask storage by renting out their own backyards.

We don't have to worry about damaging the earth, air, and water. The earth will still be here if we poison ourselves out of existence. The wind doesn't care if it is blowing radioactive dust. The rivers will flow even if they are glowing, even if there is no one here to see them.

It's not too far from casks to caskets.

But until I am in a casket, I will continue to travel and meet people.

On some trips we have to fly. We jetted to New York City. Our Camcorder jetted to Baltimore with someone else's luggage. Northwest Airlines did a good job of tracking us down to return the Camcorder. I'm going to get a T-shirt made that says, "My Camcorder went to Baltimore and all I got was this lousy baggage claim check."

My wife Pat and I were invited to the National Museum of the American Indian. It is part of the Smithsonian and is located in the George Gustav Heye Center near the southern end of Manhattan Island.

We met a lot of museum employees but I can remember only a few names. I hope they don't have a quiz. Maria Brown is the director of the program that brought us to the city. She welcomed us and showed us where we would be working. Maria also gave us a tour of the museum. We saw some bandolier bags that were on display. The beauty of the beadwork made me proud to be an Anishinaabe. I wanted to grab the tourists walking by and say, "Those were made by my people."

Another museum employee was Clinton Eliot, a Shinnob who has relatives in Wisconsin. We went outside for a smoke and to throw Ojibwe words back and forth.

While standing on the front steps, we noticed a film crew shooting in Bowling Green Park, right in front of us. It wasn't too long before a production assistant came up and asked us to move because we were in the background of their shot. While walking over to the side of the steps, I told Clinton, "This has happened before. Shinnobs have to move out of the way for the white man."

We laughed and continued visiting. Another crew member told us we hadn't moved far enough. We told him we were not moving anymore. The crew member told us they paid fifteen hundred dollars a day to film there. Clinton said, "That is the way of the white man. It always comes down to money."

We smoked and spoke Ojibwe until we were good and ready to move.

At the museum, our work was the same thing we would be doing if we were home; we made baskets. In addition to working on the baskets, we explained to the tourists who came to the museum what we were doing. We answered questions that immediately went beyond baskets to racism, gambling, treaty rights, and life on the Reservation.

We had a good time at the museum demonstrating how we make baskets. I think the visiting tourists learned that Anishinaabeg people are still here, still living our lives with the seasons. I think the museum and its workers learned also. The museum decided to add one of our baskets to their collection.

Clinton Eliot showed us how to navigate New York's subway system. He took us to the American Indian Community House. We met Indians there and got the fifty-cent tour. It felt good knowing there was such a place for Indians in the city.

After that visit, we were navigating by ourselves. We were waiting to cross a street when sure enough, we met another Shinnob. I spotted his mugshot in the sea of surrounding faces. While standing on the street corner visiting we learned that he was from Winnipeg, Canada. The Shinnob knew where the Fond du Lac Reservation was and also had heard of the village of Sawyer. When I asked him why he had left Canada, all he said was, "Warrants."

We were on our way to a bowl of soup so we invited him along. I am always amazed at the way we Shinnobs find each other in a crowd. Before we parted, he put the arm on me for a couple of bucks just before I could put the arm on him for a couple of bucks. It was a good feeling to share a meal with another Shinnob.

Pat and I rode the ferry to Staten Island and I don't know why. I don't think I know anyone there. I do know it was cooler on the water than in the concrete canyons of Manhattan.

We took pictures of Ellis Island where so many immigrants came through. The place looked like a prison or boarding school. The Statue of Liberty was standing in the bay, holding up the torch and law books. Miss Liberty looks a lot thinner since they took the scaffolding off. Her teeth and the rest of her are still green and she gets lit up at night. My cousin, Rathide, calls her the

Bitch in the Bay because she symbolizes the immigrants that overran this place now called America.

When we got to Staten Island, we turned around and boarded the return ferry. Pat and I knew we were seeing things we had only read about before. We continued playing the part of tourists and explored Times Square. We took pictures of the tourists taking pictures.

A cab driver wanted our autographs on a ten-dollar bill. I signed as Kevin Costner and I believe my wife used Pocahontas.

During an afternoon smoke break in Bowling Green Park, we saw a man grazing in the garbage cans. He would rummage around until he found a half-eaten sandwich. While talking to himself, he would shovel the food in and move on to the next garbage can. There was another man collecting aluminum cans from the garbage cans. The can man and I stayed out of the way as the hungry man continued looking for food. I would have bought him some food but he didn't look like he was in the same world as us.

I was happy to get back to the woods of Minnesota after we jetted across the United States. Sometimes I don't have to travel that far to meet someone interesting.

Through a friend of a friend, we got tickets to the George Carlin performance in Duluth. Herb O'Brien, an old friend of George Carlin, got the tickets. He then took us backstage to meet George Carlin before the performance.

Carlin is a master storyteller. He told us a story about getting arrested with Herb and Lenny Bruce in Chicago. They all went to jail because an underage girl was in the audience. Carlin talked fondly of his wife, Brenda, and daughter, Kelly. He praised Brenda for sticking with him all these years. I was saddened earlier this year when I heard of Brenda's death.

George Carlin said he thinks Indians should be identified by their tribal names instead of the generic Native
American term. This Shinnob agreed with him. He did
think my term American Americans was acceptable.

During the nearly two-hour performance, George
Carlin told jokes at the rate of ten a minute with gusts
up to twenty-five. He tells jokes about things that people only dare to think about.

Some weeks later I got a call from a man identifying
himself as George Carlin. I just knew it was my cousin,
Butch Martineau, trying to trick me. After a while the
voice on the phone convinced me I was talking with
George Carlin. He had read the review I wrote about his
performance. He tracked me down through the editor of
the paper that carried my column. He just called to say
thanks. I thanked him for his thanks.

Sometimes we have to travel a bit farther to meet interesting people.

Patricia and I motored to the Chicago area so I could
recite poetry. Sandy Lyon organized the event for her
group called Anishinaabe Niijii. She gave me a copy of
her poem called "Wet Dreamcatcher."

The event was a reception following a concert by Bonnie Raitt. It was held in a large tent on the grounds of
Poplar Creek Theater where Raitt was performing. After
singing, she came to the tent to meet the fans.

Bonnie Raitt is a gracious woman who helps American Indian causes. She was in the Twin Cities helping
the people in their struggle against killer wastes at
Prairie Island. I heard she also did a benefit for the
White Earth Land Recovery Project, Winona LaDuke's
organization that is getting the land back on the White
Earth Reservation in northern Minnesota.

Because of the schedule, they wanted me to read only

one poem. I told them it would be silly to recite just one poem after driving five hundred miles in a Rez car. I recited two of the poems from my book, *Walking the Rez Road*. After reciting, I gave Bonnie Raitt my autograph in the book.

She hugged me and I hugged her back. My wife later said it looked like I was hugging too enthusiastically. Up close, Bonnie Raitt has crinkly blue, blue eyes that seem to look deep inside. She is slender, about as skinny as a turn signal, like my cousin, Rathide, would say. She has big hair.

Bonnie Raitt continued walking around the tent visiting with people. When she came by where we were standing, she told Pat she had a "cool husband." Pat said, "I know."

I had to agree with both of these women and we posed for a picture together. To keep peace in the family, I am not going to buy any more Bonnie Raitt tapes or CDs.

As I travel about, I see the need to change and adapt to survive in the world we now occupy, the new world of technology that is around us every day.

We need to put our electronic moccasin tracks on the information superhighway. There is an information revolution going on and if we don't join, we'll be left in the dust. I remember the words of Crow Chief Plenty Coups: "With education, you are the white man's equal, without it, you are the white man's victim."

My dream is to see gambling profits used to put a computer in every home on the Rez. Not just a computer but access to the information networks also. The Shinnobs on the Rez would have access to information.

Computer users in the world could learn about Shinnobs, since the highway is a two-way street. Further, the computers on the Rez could be linked together.

Say, for example, the leaders wanted to sell treaty rights to the state of Minnesota. The Shinnobs could use their machines to discuss the issue. After the discussion, the people could vote on the treaty sale. The leaders could be part of the discussion and give their reasons for selling. Or perhaps the leaders wanted to get in a casino deal with the city of Duluth. Once again, the people could be heard.

Using computers in this way would lead to pure democracy instead of the way we do it now with *Robert's Rules of Order.* We could vote on every important issue and become computer literate in one generation. Our children will be better prepared for the world they will live in.

Anishinaabeg have a long history of adapting to new technology. The gun replaced the bow for hunting. Steel knives last longer than stone ones and are easier to sharpen. Telephones and police scanners have made the moccasin telegraph more efficient. The big and little satellite dishes can be found everywhere on the Rez. They have sprouted and now all look like they're praying to a god in the southern sky. Nowadays, we play more blackjack than cribbage.

What sound did an early Rez computer make?

15-2,15-4, 15-6, and a pair is 8.

The children of the Rez are learning about computers in school but they would learn more with a machine at home. The young ones could teach the old ones how to use the new technology.

Once on the http://www highway, the Shinnobs could share information with computer users all over the world. My travels have taught me there is a thirst for information about the Anishinaabeg.

Maintaining the information network would create jobs. We'd need technicians and librarians, computer geeks and administrators to keep the whole system running.

The people could exchange community service hours for hardware, software, and access.

We have the technology. Computers are already in use in the schools, the casinos, and administrative offices but we need to bring them to the people. We just need to convince our leaders that connecting the people to computers is a good idea. (Shinnobs can't afford to be hitchhikers on the http://www highway.)

As I travel the highways of America, I always meet people who are eager to prove their Indian connection. Why do so many people want to be Indian?

I was in Madison, Wisconsin, attending a reading by Anishinaabe poet, Kim Blaeser. She was reading from her book, *Trailing You*. After the reading, while Kim was talking with her fans and signing books, I stepped outside to have a smoke.

A woman I never saw before came up and asked if I were an Indian. When I told her I was Anishinaabe, she started telling me of her Indian connection. She said she was part Cherokee on her mother's side. It was a deep, dark, family secret. I murmured sympathetic noises during her sad tale of child abuse, neglect, and denial. The conversation was barely minutes old and I was already hearing terrible family secrets. I didn't know what to say to ease this woman's pain.

The conversation left me troubled. Why did she think I could help her find the answers to the questions she was asking?

Then I remembered, this has happened quite a few times before.

I was walking out of a building in Minneapolis. A man walked up and asked if I were Indian. I told him I was Anishinaabe. He started off by telling me how the Indians respected the land just like his brother had. The white man then went into a long, convoluted story about his brother, the hunter.

When the hunter brother died, they cremated him, loaded him into shotgun shells, and scattered him over the land. It was a fitting memorial for a hunter who loved the land like the Indians.

The man was getting misty eyed as he told me the story of his brother. I don't know why I was selected to hear the dead brother story. As I was walking away from the conversation, I remembered wanting to ask if they hit anything with their brother.

My friends and relatives tell me the same thing happens to them as they travel. We trade stories back and forth about the white people anxious to prove their Indian connection.

It is usually Cherokee but I have noticed a new trend. Now people are claiming to be Blackfeet, Dakota, or even Anishinaabe. So why is this happening? It can't be the gambling gold because people have been trying to prove their Indian connections since before the casinos opened. Maybe the people sense our feeling of being connected to a family.

I know we are rooted here. We have been here a long time and we prefer to live together. In my small village, I am related to about half the people that live here. I bask in the security of living among family. For example, I ran into my brother, Russ, at the Sawyer store. I told him if it gets any colder, I will have to start wearing long johns. He laughed and said he has had his on for a month now.

A small connection, but a reminder that we are all in this together. Living among family isn't always a happy utopia. We have the usual collection of oddballs, misfits, and those not flying in formation. But my sister, Jean Dufault, just graduated from the University of Minnesota–Duluth. She will be teaching at a school on the Rez, her way of paying back for the gifts she was given.

The feeling of family can't be bought with money.

I was waiting in an airport for my airplane ride back home. I was reading my newspaper while waiting for the flight to be called. I felt like someone was staring at me. I looked up and saw a small boy looking directly at me. He looked to be about the same age as my grandson, Ezigaa. He had black hair, brown skin, and brown eyes. His mother came up, grabbed his hand, and told him not to stare.

She asked if I were an Indian. I told her I was an Anishinaabe. She said her son was an Indian too, maybe Lakota, maybe something else. The woman went into great detail about the adoption process that allowed her to have this child. She further explained how they take their son to a lot of powwows so he can be proud of his heritage. I wanted to tell her that there was a lot more to it than powwows but my plane was loading. I smiled at the boy like he was my grandson. He smiled back.

On my way home, I felt sorry for that little Lakota, maybe something else, boy that would be growing up in a white home.

I like traveling because I get to go home at the end of the trip. Every time I come home, I realize how fortunate I am to live where I do. Another flight took me over the Atlantic Ocean.

We were not exactly innocents, but we went abroad anyway. My wife Pat and I were invited to Aberdeen, Scotland, to meet Scottish people who wished to learn about life on the Rez. When my cousin, Rathide, heard about the trip, he wanted me to see if they were still making white people over there.

The plane ride was long and boring. I liked the boring part of the flight. The DC-10 cruised through the air at 550 miles per hour. It was 41 below on the other side of the cabin wall. I didn't want to know the windchill. The Atlantic was under my feet, five or six miles under.

We landed at Gatwick, the airport south of London. We took a little train to a big train at Kings Cross Station. London was on the other side of the train windows. The big train took us through the middle of English history north to Scotland. The senior conductor on the train sounded like a cast member in a British movie as he announced the towns.

The trees in the English countryside looked kind of scrawny compared to northern Minnesota. Most of the trees had green moss on the trunks and branches. Robin

Hood would have had a hell of a time hiding from the Sheriff of Nottingham in those woods.

We passed through a belt of nuclear power plants. I was immediately reminded of the killer wastes at Prairie Island back in Minnesota. The cars and trucks were driving on the other side of the road compared to back home. It looked like all the drivers were in on it.

After an eight-hour train ride, we arrived in Aberdeen. When I got off the train, I noticed they have dark there just like we do at home. We were met by the members of the Association of Native American Tribes. The group spends time educating Scottish people on Native issues. Sure enough, we began meeting Shinnobs.

Rose Porter from the Fond du Lac Reservation was there to meet us. She lives in Aberdeen with her husband, Dave. Debbie Picotte lives in Aberdeen also. She has relatives in Minnesota and Nebraska. We shook hands and smiled at the rest of the members.

It was damp and cold, unlike the dry cold in Minnesota. I was glad I had my moosehide mitts along. Two association members gave us a ride to the flat (apartment) we would be using while there.

The ride to the flat was in a little car through narrow, wet streets. I was sitting in the front seat with the driver to my right. We actually went out and drove in the streets where the traffic was coming at me. I was unarmed: I didn't have a steering wheel, brakes, or horn. It was scary at first but I got used to it. But when I got used to that, they gave me a new one—traffic circles. There are five or more roads converging at a circle. The cars get on the circle and then get off at the road they want. Somehow it all works and we got to the flat with fenders intact.

In the Granite City of Aberdeen, we stayed in a granite apartment building. The rooms were small and the wood floor had a squeak. The floor sound was at first romantic but got annoying before long. The flat didn't have a TV; what freedom, I thought. After riding in a car, an airplane, a train, and a car for twenty-four hours we were tired. My wife and I had car, jet, train lag so we slept like we'd been clubbed.

The next morning we crawled out of bed to crawl around a genuine Scottish castle with our new friends. Dunnottar Castle is right on the North Sea. I felt like we were in a postcard. The white sheep grazing on the green grass, the stonework castle with the troubled North Sea behind, the sea birds, all made me want to take out my camera. We felt the rain falling sideways in the wind. This was a castle like I had read about. It even had a dungeon where 140 people were confined during one of the wars. There was a man visiting the castle with his bagpipe. He played his music but our local guides informed us he was not very good. It sounded great to me, maybe it was the setting. The castle felt dead. We admired the stonework but were happy to leave. It was a nice place to visit but I wouldn't want to live in a dungeon there. After seeing the sheep again, we traded sheep jokes with our local guides.

Pat and I were there to talk about life on the Rez. We spoke to many groups of Scottish people. We found them in libraries, at a Friends meeting, a writers' group, a women's center, in museums, at a Spiritualist Church, at Marischal College Museum, and in schools. We were interviewed by BBC Scotland. I think I told them everything I know. The people had a real hunger for information about us.

We went to a nice place to eat with the association members. Before the main course, I decided to use the bathroom (loo, water closet). I asked a civilian for directions and found the two doors. The international symbols were on the doors. One symbol wore pants and the other wore a skirt. I was in Scotland, land of the kilt. I couldn't decide which was the one for me. Finally, in desperation, I chose one. It was the right choice. While in there I noticed the toilet flushing handle was on the other side. I did an informal check and found it was universal. The toilet flushing handles were like the traffic, both on the opposite side. I told my wife about this but she didn't think it was significant.

We traded wild rice for haggis. That dish tastes like corned beef hash with a lot of pepper. I had seconds. Haggis used to be cooked in a sheep's stomach but I don't think they do that anymore. There was a whitish-looking food that I thought tasted like potatoes. Our host informed us we were eating mashed potatoes with butter. The bacon was lean and I couldn't get a decent bit of grease off it for our morning oatmeal (porridge). Among the Anishinaabeg, bacon grease and oatmeal is considered the Breakfast of Champions.

We learned about Scotland when we weren't talking. They have old history compared to the United States. We visited stone circles that were erected thousands of years ago. They were built so they could be seen from another stone circle on the next hill. A message could be passed from one hilltop to another all the way across the country. I called it an early Internet.

The Highlanders have a history similar to our own. They were thrown off their land, their homes were torn down, they couldn't speak their language and were treated as something less than human. Thousands of Scottish people came to Canada and the United States during the Clearances.

Marlene Forsythe, one of the association's officers, offered to be our tour guide when we had a scheduled free day. She drove her little car through the Grampian Mountains. M, as she came to be named, must be related to Richard Petty or some other race car driver. She drove the narrow roads like a moonshiner. We leaped at a chance to crawl around another castle because we could get out of the car for a while.

M took us to Glenfiddich Distillery where we learned a little about whiskey making. Single malt Scotch is distilled and bottled there. Whiskey making goes on night and day here, with warehouses full of Scotch, just waiting to be old enough to drink. The place was a chemical dependency counselor's nightmare. It didn't look like a good place to hold an AA meeting. At the end of the tour, I had a wee dram (water glass) of Glenfiddich.

After we survived the drive, M took us to Black Isle where we met her Mum (mother). We spent the night at her croft (small farm). Each room had a wee fireplace. The next morning M drove us to Inverness and Loch Ness. Along the way we looked at the birch trees. It didn't look like the kind of bark we use in our baskets.

Of course we had to look for Nessie. Our first stop was at the Official Loch Ness Monster Exhibition Centre where we got an overview of Nessie. Locals have long been telling stories about the animal that lives in the loch (lake). Some of the stories are fourteen hundred years old.

We went to look. Loch Ness is a long, skinny lake. We watched a rainstorm coming up the loch. The colors of the sky included some I couldn't name. I could hardly wait to get home to show my family what I was seeing.

Pat and I were ready for Nessie. The Camcorder battery was fully charged, it had a fresh cassette. The 35mm camera was loaded with high-speed, color-print film. We waited, then we saw Nessie.

The animal was traveling incognito up the loch ahead of the rainstorm. It was about five hundred yards offshore. The animal had cleverly fashioned a disguise that looked exactly like a fishing boat. We watched, took pictures, and marveled at the realism of the disguise. What a piece of work. It looked exactly like a fishing boat right down to the motor *putt-putting* along. We weren't fooled. We took pictures of the Loch Ness Monster.

The Scottish people, including M, spoke a different English than we did. I was about a whole sentence behind the entire time in Scotland. I had to constantly ask people to repeat what they had said. They understood us just fine. I think American movies and television have helped.

I learned how to speak the local language enough to say, "Aye, I'll have another wee dram of that single malt." ("Yes, give me another drink of that scotch.)

Overall, I think we learned more about the Scottish people than they learned about us.

Our time in Scotland was over too soon but we looked forward to the twenty-four hours in London. The train once again took us through English history. We saw a castle in Edinburgh, the Firth of Forth, coal cars in Newcastle, and English people *(zhaaganaashag)*.

We toured a little part of London but we were thinking of home. We saw Buckingham Palace but the guard wasn't changing. I don't think the queen was home, she probably didn't know we were going to be in town. We rode the train back to Gatwick Airport. Our plane was waiting for us.

The airplane took us over Ireland, by Iceland, and across Greenland. When I saw Hudson Bay, I knew we were getting close. The plane landed in Minneapolis where we joined our family. Patricia and I went home, happy to be breathing the air on the Fond du Lac Reservation. I knew I was home as soon as I drank that first dipper *(gwaaba'igan)* of Sawyer water. The first hug from my grandson, Ezigaa, proved that I was back with family.

Ezigaa wanted to know, where had we been? I think I will have plenty of stories to tell him about where I have been. I will have time to tell him stories as we live our lives with the seasons, making syrup, making rice, making baskets and memories. I will tell him stories so he can tell his grandchildren. Now that boy wants to know if the Creator *(gichi-manidoo)* is a man or woman. The questions and answers, like the Anishinaabeg, go on and on and on. *Mii saw iw.*

Jim Northrup is a member of the Ojibwe people and lives on the Fond du Lac Reservation in northern Minnesota. He is the author of *Walking the Rez Road*, and his monthly column "The Fond du Lac Follies" appears in several Native American newspapers.